Jack Hayford and Dick Eastman

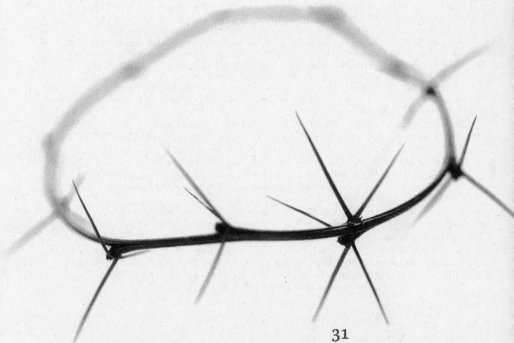

31
Days Meditating
on the
Majesty
of Jesus

TYNDALE HOUSE PUBLISHERS, INC., CAROL STREAM, ILLINOIS

TYNDALE and Tyndale's quill logo are registered trademarks of Tyndale House Publishers, Inc.

31 Days Meditating on the Majesty of Jesus

Copyright © 1988, 2007 by Dick Eastman and Jack Hayford. All rights reserved.

Cover photograph © 2006 by Gavin Kingcome/Jupiter Images. All rights reserved.

Designed by Stephen Vosloo

Edited by Bonne Steffen

Previously published in 1988 as *Living & Praying In Jesus' Name* by Tyndale House Publishers, Inc. (ISBN 0-8423-2667-7).

The authors wish to gratefully acknowledge several primary reference sources that were especially helpful in the preparation of this book. We also wish to express our gratitude for the kind permission of the publishers to quote freely from the pages of these resources: From *The Search for God,* by David Manning White, copyright 1983. Reprinted by permission of Macmillan Publishing Company. From *Eerdman's Book of Famous Prayers,* by Veronica Zunel, copyright 1983. Reprinted by permission of Wm. B. Eerdmans Publishing Company. From *All the Divine Names and Titles in the Bible,* by Herbert Lockyer, copyright 1975. Reprinted by permission of Zondervan.

Scripture quotations are taken from the *Holy Bible,* New Living Translation, copyright © 1996, 2004. Used by permission of Tyndale House Publishers, Inc., Carol Stream, Illinois 60188. All rights reserved.

Scripture quotations marked KJV are taken from the *Holy Bible,* King James Version.

Scripture quotations marked NIV are taken from the *Holy Bible,* New International Version®. NIV®. Copyright © 1973, 1978, 1984 by International Bible Society. Used by permission of Zondervan. All rights reserved.

Scripture quotations marked "NKJV™" are taken from the New King James Version®. Copyright © 1982 by Thomas Nelson, Inc. Used by permission. All rights reserved.

Scripture quotations marked TLB are taken from *The Living Bible,* copyright © 1971. Used by permission of Tyndale House Publishers, Inc., Carol Stream, Illinois 60188. All rights reserved.

Scripture quotations marked AMP are taken from *The Amplified Bible.* Old Testament copyright © 1965, 1987 by The Zondervan Corporation. *The Amplified New Testament* copyright © 1958, 1987 by The Lockman Foundation. Used by permission.

ISBN: 978-0-7394-8096-0

Printed in the United States of America

To him who sits on the throne and to the Lamb
be praise and honor and glory and power, for ever and ever!

Revelation 5:13, NIV

Write your blessed name, O Lord, upon my heart,
there to remain so indelibly engraved, that no prosperity,
no adversity shall ever move me from your love.
Be to me a strong tower of defense,
a comforter in tribulation, a deliverer in distress,
a very present help in trouble, and a guide to heaven
through the many temptations and dangers of this life.

Thomas à Kempis

Contents

Foreword

Royalty and all it entails fascinates everyone. It surely did me, as its evidence was everywhere present when I was on a month-long trip to the British Isles a few years ago. In between my speaking engagements, there was plenty of time for my wife, Anna, and me to explore London, the back roads of the Cotswolds, the rustic lanes of Wales, and the hills of Scotland, among other stops along the way. We couldn't avoid the prominence of royalty or regal influences wherever we traveled. It caught our attention on a daily basis because it so broadly defined the British history which surrounded us.

Britain's one thousand years of "kingdom" existence marks the landscape there—here, a monument to a long-past victory; there, a milestone marking a decisive battle; other places, a grand gate or arch commemorating an achievement, a returning conqueror, or a royal wedding. Majesty seemed to be everywhere! And it was on one of those days—amid these scenes—that God's Holy Spirit ignited this song's melody and lyrics in my soul about an even greater King:

MAJESTY! WORSHIP HIS MAJESTY!

UNTO JESUS BE ALL GLORY, POWER, AND PRAISE.

MAJESTY! KINGDOM AUTHORITY

FLOWS FROM HIS THRONE UNTO HIS OWN

WHO HIS ANTHEM RAISE.

SO EXALT—LIFT UP ON HIGH—THE NAME OF JESUS!

MAGNIFY—COME GLORIFY CHRIST JESUS THE KING!

MAJESTY! WORSHIP HIS MAJESTY!

JESUS WHO DIED, NOW GLORIFIED,

KING OF ALL KINGS.

© 1981 BRENTWOOD BENSON MUSIC, NASHVILLE

The sights, sounds, and surroundings we encountered brought recurring thoughts of our Savior, Jesus Christ—the regal glory of our King. He is the timeless Victor in battle; Jesus, the Conqueror at Calvary, Who will return in even greater triumph. Jesus, Heaven's Lover and royal Bridegroom, Who will return to be united with His redeemed at the ultimate Royal Wedding. Yes, Britain's millennium of earthly rule is indeed but a day with Him, but it nonetheless holds promises of a future time when His Majesty, Jesus Christ, shall have His day—reigning supreme as King!

Jesus' Kingdom and kingliness is eternal. His name defines His person, His grace, His gift of Himself, His abiding love, His truly awe-inspiring character. That's what these pages contain: an invitation to a month-long journey of focusing your thoughts and drawing your heart to explore the depths of the royal wonder found in the Name of Jesus.

His is the one Name that is declared high and above every other name.
His is the one Name by which we may be saved and enter eternal life.

There's nobody else like Jesus. In these pages, Dick Eastman and I have provided you with an introduction to the wondrous experience that thirty-one days of meditating on the majesty of Jesus can bring. You'll encounter hundreds of terms, titles, and themes which both the Scriptures and the saints of the ages have used to describe Jesus. When you see the exceeding beauty of His Majesty there is but one response: *Worship Him!*

When was the last time you worshipped the Lord Jesus Christ as Your Majesty?

That's the objective of this book—to *think* on Him, then to *thank* Him. As you get to know Jesus better through these meditations, I pray that you'll be the recipient of a wisdom wiser than this world knows, and you'll be enriched with a wealth that can never be taken from you.

In Jesus' Majestic Name,

Jack W. Hayford

President, The Foursquare Church
Chancellor, The King's College and Seminary
Founding Pastor, The Church On The Way
Van Nuys, California

Introduction

A friend asked Mrs. Albert Einstein if she understood the theory of relativity. "No, not at all," she answered. Then she added with a chuckle, "But I understand Albert, and he can be trusted!"

It's doubtful any phrase used in our prayers is said more frequently, or understood less, than the expression "in Jesus' name."

Yet our capacity to trust the Lord is clearly linked in Scripture to our knowledge of His name. The psalmist said, "Those who know your name trust in you, for you, O LORD, do not abandon those who search for you" (Psalm 9:10). "You are my King and my God. You command victories for Israel. Only by your power can we push back our enemies; only in your name can we trample our foes" (Psalm 44:4-5).

In the New Testament, Jesus extended a certain "power of attorney" to His disciples—the authority to use His name in transacting business on His behalf. He said, "You can ask for anything in my name, and I will do it, so that the Son can bring glory to the Father" (John 14:13).

But how do we apply all this in practical terms as we endeavor to live and pray today "in Jesus' name"? The author of Proverbs hints at an answer when he declares, "The name of the LORD is a strong fortress; the godly run to him and are safe" (Proverbs 18:10).

Living and praying in Jesus' name means much more than merely saying a phrase at the end of a prayer. It is to begin each new day empowered by a truth of Jesus that is found in one of His names. It is focusing on a specific characteristic embodied in that name, which ultimately helps us understand Who Jesus is.

All of us have names. The dictionary defines *name* as "a word or words by which an entity is designated and distinguished from others." Nineteenth century missionary and spiritually encouraging author Andrew Murray amplifies this thought:

What is a person's name? It is a word or expression in which a person is represented to us. When I mention or hear a name, it brings to mind the whole man, what I know of him, and also the impression he has made on me. The name of a king includes his honor, his power, his kingdom. His name is the symbol of his power. And so each name of God embodies and represents some part of the glory of the Unseen One. The name of Christ is the expression of everything he has done and everything he is and lives to do as our Mediator.[1]

Every name and title you'll read in this book applies specifically and directly to Jesus Christ. Some descriptions occur in the Old Testament as titles of God, "for in Christ lives all the fullness of God in a human body" (Colossians 2:9). The apostle Paul also wrote, "For God was in Christ, reconciling the world to himself . . ." (2 Corinthians 5:19), while Jesus' disciple John begins his Gospel with, "The Word [Christ] was God" and "The Word [Christ/God] became human" (John 1:1, 14) and later records Jesus' words: "Anyone who has seen me has seen the Father!" (John 14:9). The three members of the Godhead—Father, Son, and Holy Spirit—are not competitive or confused. The Father in all His fullness is pleased to live in Christ, and the Holy Spirit brings Christ glory (Colossians 1:19; John 16:14).

This book contains thirty-one names or titles of Jesus, one for each day of the month. Each chapter presents a theme with a key word that sums up a specific name. You will also read prayers (both ancient and contemporary) that give you more insight into the name you're reading about. And at the end of each devotional, you'll find a list of related names (which are referenced in the index) to expand your biblical knowledge of Who Jesus Christ is and what He has done personally for you.

Dick Eastman

INTERNATIONAL PRESIDENT
EVERY HOME FOR CHRIST
COLORADO SPRINGS, COLORADO

No one has ever seen God. But the one and only Son is himself God and is near to the Father's heart. He has revealed God to us.

JOHN 1:18

1 {COMFORT}

The Lord of Peace

Now may the Lord of peace himself give you his peace at all times and in every situation. The Lord be with you all. 2 Thessalonians 3:16

How often do you long for peace in your life?

St. Ignatius Loyola when compiling his *Spiritual Exercises* wrote: "In times of dryness and desolation we must be patient, and wait with resignation for the return of consolation, putting our trust in the goodness of God. We must animate ourselves by the thought that God is always with us, that He only allows this trial for our greater good, and that we have not necessarily lost His grace because we have lost the taste and feeling of it."[1]

Comfort or consolation flows from God's divine nature. He not only possesses peace, His very nature is peace. Even in those times when we may "have lost the taste and feeling" of God's grace, His grace still abounds.

Sometimes Satan tries to convince us that God has abandoned us. But remember that Satan (the devil) is the "father of lies" (John 8:44). God may, indeed, be silent at times, but He is always there. He feels every hurt and senses every pain we endure. If you know the Lord, you will know peace, for Jesus Christ is the Lord of Peace.

Knowing His Name

When Paul concluded his second letter to the Christians in Thessalonica he added this benediction, "Now may the Lord of peace himself give you his peace at all times and in every situation. The Lord be with you all" (2 Thessalonians 3:16).

According to Paul, there are three unique things about God's peace: its intimacy, constancy, and supremacy.

First, notice *the intimacy of this peace*. The Lord Himself promises to give peace. Jesus doesn't use an angelic messenger to deliver His promise. He does it Himself—a picture of personal intimacy.

Second, note *the constancy of this peace*. "The Lord . . . give you his peace at all times." We all experience unpredictable turns in our lives that cause turmoil, strife, and distress. But Paul says that at every point God's peace will prevail. That's a picture of true constancy.

Finally, consider *the supremacy of this peace*. "The Lord . . . give you peace in every situation." This is no ordinary peace; it is

"peace supreme." For every troubling situation we may encounter, our Creator provides His own unique "measure of peace" for that specific circumstance.

2 Corinthians 1:3 says, "All praise to God, the Father of our Lord Jesus Christ. God is our merciful Father and the source of all comfort." Mercy and comfort are not merely promised, they are insured in and through the One who offers them from His endless supply. Think of it this way: There will never be a shortage of either mercy or comfort; there will never be a restriction. God has the monopoly on them both!

Living His Name

The Greek word for peace, *eireney,* implies unity or wholeness. When that sense of inner unity is broken, it is "unpeaceful." But in three different ways, Christ, our Lord of Peace, restores brokenness with His breath of wholeness.

First, *Jesus breathes calm into troubled situations*. Consider the unforgettable words Christ spoke

God not only possesses peace, His very nature is peace.

to a raging storm: "Silence! Be still!" (Mark 4:39). His authority over creation was magnificently displayed, to the awe and wonder of His frightened disciples.

"Who is this man?" they asked each other. "Even the wind and waves obey him!" (Mark 4:41). Not only was there immediate calm, there was a lasting tranquility.

Second, *Jesus breathes unity into troubled situations*. "Our friendship with God was restored by the death of his Son," Paul tells us (Romans 5:10). In Jesus' name we have been joined to God's heart. We not only have a Savior who calms the storms of life, but in Christ we have an anchor of hope that secures us in a safe harbor (Hebrews 6:19).

Finally, *Jesus breathes reconciliation into troubled situations*. Paul wrote, "For Christ himself has brought peace to us" (Ephesians 2:14). The grace we have received from God can change our attitude toward others. The Lord of Peace works in and through us to bring reconciliation in difficult situations. Ephesians 2:14-17 details Jesus Christ's pivotal role in breaking down the wall of hostility—whether it be a wall of racism, religious dissension, or cultural differences. We

are not only called to love one another in Jesus' name, but we are given a resource for reconciliation through prayer.

Praying His Name

When we pray in Jesus' name, the Lord of Peace, we bring His peace and comfort into each potentially trouble-filled situation. It doesn't guarantee that things will change the way we want them to. God's specific purpose for bringing difficulty into our lives may be to make us long for more of Jesus, our Lord of Peace. Our prayers not only flood our spirits with peace, but more important, the prayers summon the presence of Christ, Who is our Peace, to fill us.

As you call upon the Lord of Peace, you are accessing God's divine rest. You can pray expectantly as reflected in the poet Christina Rossetti's nineteenth-century prayer:

O Lord, Jesus Christ, who art as the shadow of a great rock in a weary land, who beholdest Thy weak creatures weary of labor, weary of pleasure, weary of hope deferred, weary of self; in thine abundant compassion, and fellow feeling with us, and unutterable tenderness, bring us, we pray Thee, unto Thy rest.[2]

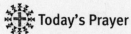 **Today's Prayer**

HELP, LORD! MY WORLD TODAY SEEMS LIKE GALILEE AT TEMPEST TIME. I FEEL VERY SMALL—MY BOAT IS PAPER-THIN AND THE WAVES ARE STEEL SCISSORS. TODAY I UNDERSTAND THE DISCIPLES CRY: "MASTER—DON'T YOU CARE THAT WE'RE SINKING?" FORGIVE MY FEARS, MY FAITHLESSNESS. I COME TO YOU BELIEVING: YOU, LORD JESUS CHRIST, ARE THE LORD OF PEACE. I TURN TO YOU AND AWAY FROM THE STORM. I LOOK TO YOU AND AWAY FROM FEAR. TODAY I STEP INTO THE RESOURCES OF YOUR NAME—PRINCE OF PEACE. IN YOUR ALMIGHTY NAME I WELCOME CALMNESS, WHOLENESS, AND HARMONY. PRAISE YOUR NAME, LORD JESUS. AMEN.

MY PERSONAL MEDITATIONS

_____

_____

_____

_____

_____

_____

_____

_____

_____

MORE NAMES FOR JESUS

Check the index beginning on page 162 for these additional names for Jesus that suggest the Lord of Peace: Bringer of Peace; God of Love and Peace; Great Shepherd of the Sheep; Jehovah-Shalom: The Lord Is Peace; Prince of Peace; True Place of Rest.

Wonderful Counselor

For a child is born to us, a son is given to us. The government will rest on his shoulders. And he will be called: Wonderful Counselor, Mighty God, Everlasting Father, Prince of Peace. Isaiah 9:6

Is God the first person you go to when you need counsel?

When it came to mathematics and languages at Cambridge University, Henry Martyn was brilliant. In 1806, Martyn left for India as chaplain for the East India Company with the goal of translating the New Testament into Hindi. During the next six years of his life (before an untimely death at thirty-one), Martyn completed that God-directed assignment, then did the same with a Persian New Testament before undertaking a revision of an Arabic New Testament. Yet as talented as Martyn was, he experienced times of deep frustration with the projects. At those moments, Henry Martyn cried out to the Lord for insight. With simplicity and candor Martyn prayed:

Lord, I am blind and helpless, stupid and ignorant.
Cause me to hear; Cause me to know;
Teach me to do; Lead me.[1]

As Martyn pored over the Scriptures, he noticed that a considerable number of biblical prayers were not requests for material blessings but for spiritual insight. The psalmist, for example, repeatedly prayed "Show me," "Lead me," "Teach me," "Direct me," "Instruct me," and "Guide me." The apostle Paul also was not hesitant to include similar reminders in his personal prayers. To the Colossians he wrote, "So we have not stopped praying for you since we first heard about you. We ask God to give you complete knowledge of his will and to give you spiritual wisdom and understanding" (Colossians 1:9).

Both the apostle Paul and Henry Martyn had discovered a vital secret: Praying in Jesus' name means receiving counsel and insight at the highest level, for Jesus Christ is our Wonderful Counselor!

Knowing His Name

Have you ever listened to Handel's *Messiah*? One of the most joyous songs contains a list of prophetic names describing the future Messiah, Jesus Christ, as proclaimed by Isaiah. One of those names is Wonderful Counselor (Isaiah 9:6). Isaiah is foretelling of the One Who will be the ultimate answer to Israel's every problem. At the time of the prophecy, the kingdom of Judah was in desperate need of a ruler who would be able to provide "wise counsel" for mounting troubling situations.

We all find ourselves on occasion facing problems that defy solutions. But in Jesus' name, our Wonderful Counselor, we can find help.

Franz Delitzsch, a Hebrew scholar, notes how the seventy translators of the Septuagint (the Greek translation of the Old Testament from the Hebrew) joined the two words Wonderful Counselor in their translation, literally describing Christ as the "One counseling wonderful things." An alternative translation renders it "a wonder of a counselor." Essentially, Christ embodies both a wonder-working essence (that is, a person filled with wonders, a person "wonderful" in His own right) and the counsel of heavenly origin which, when combined, bring divine insight into human difficulties.

The Hebrew words translated *secret* (KJV) and *wonderful* (NKJV) are taken from the Hebrew word *pehleh* meaning "a marvel, a miracle, or a wonderful thing." The NIV translates it as "beyond understanding" (Judges 13:18) and "an amazing thing" (Judges 13:19). Interestingly, *pehleh's* primary root *pawlaw,* which means "great, marvelous, or wonderful," has a fundamental meaning of "to separate or distinguish." Obviously the idea of these words is that this title of the coming Messiah, Wonderful, is indicative of the fact that He stands out far over and above and separate from every other source of ability or counsel. There is none comparable!

And when this expression

Because **Christ sees all** *there is to see,*
His counsel is exactly what we need.

Wonderful is combined with the term *Counselor* (from the Hebrew word *yawats* meaning "to advise, resolve, or guide"), we have an exciting concept of One who gives amazing advice "beyond understanding"; One whose advice is wonder!

Living His Name

Living in Jesus' name, our Wonderful Counselor, is facing each day anticipating an inexhaustible supply of His advice from a supernatural vantage point. Because Christ sees all there is to see, His counsel, instruction, teaching, and direction are exactly what we need to navigate every circumstance.

When someone receives Christ as his or her Savior, that person is usually told that Jesus has come into his or her heart to dwell personally. Christ embodies divine insight, so as He speaks from where He lives (the hearts of believers), we must learn to listen "within" for His advice and counsel. If what we hear in our hearts is really of God, we can rest assured that His Word (Hebrews 4:12) along with the wise counsel of Spirit-led advisers (Proverbs 20:18; 15:22) will confirm it.

Praying His Name

The hymn writer Charles C. Converse wrote, "O what peace we often forfeit, O what needless pain we bear, all because we do not carry everything to God in prayer."

Insight for today is but a prayer away if you'll just learn to listen. Too many of us are like Joshua who, after seeking insight from God prior to his triumph at Jericho (Joshua 5:13-15) failed to go directly to God before what became his defeat at Ai (Joshua 7:2-5).

As we spend quality time alone with God, He will show us the day through His eyes. After all, Jesus didn't just say "pray." He said, "Watch and pray" (Matthew 26:41).

Our enemy Satan wants to defeat us by tempting us at every turn—especially targeting the most vulnerable areas of our life. Whom will we meet? Where will we go? What plans do we have? Is temptation waiting in some future hidden moment? Christ will warn us if we stay close to Him. While we are "keeping our eyes on Jesus" (Hebrews 12:2), He will be looking out for us (John 10:28).

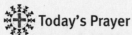
Today's Prayer

SOMEONE HAS SAID, LORD, "IT'S A JUNGLE OUT THERE." HE WAS TALKING ABOUT THIS WORLD YOU CREATED IN BEAUTY AND PERFECTION, BUT WHICH HAS DEGENERATED SO MUCH—DRAGGED DOWN WHEN WE AS HUMANKIND SINNED. DEAR LORD, THIS JUNGLE IS MY ADDRESS. I'M NOT BLAMING YOU FOR THE ANIMAL-LIKE BEHAVIOR OF PEOPLE WHO PREY ON EACH OTHER. NOR AM I COMPLAINING ABOUT THE CONFUSING SITUATIONS WHICH PREVENT A CLEAR VIEW AHEAD. I SIMPLY COME TO PRAY. I'M SO THANKFUL FOR YOU, JESUS, MY WONDERFUL COUNSELOR, WHO GIVES INSIGHT, WISDOM, PERSPECTIVE, AND KNOWLEDGE BEYOND MY OWN. TODAY AS I FACE DAILY DEMANDS, I PROCEED IN YOUR NAME, DEPENDING UPON YOU TO HELP ME KNOW WHAT TO DO AND HOW TO DO IT. IN JESUS' NAME, AMEN.

MY PERSONAL MEDITATIONS

_____

_____

_____

_____

_____

_____

_____

_____

MORE NAMES FOR JESUS

Check the index beginning on page 162 for these additional names for Jesus that suggest a Wonderful Counselor: Good Teacher; Great Light; Teacher and Lord; Wisdom of God; Word of Life.

+ Day 3 {A W A K E N I N G}
The Bright Morning Star

I, Jesus, have sent my angel to give you this message for the churches. I am both the source of David and the heir to his throne. I am the bright morning star.

Revelation 22:16

Have you ever experienced a wake-up call in your life that impacted you from that moment on?

In *Nine Lectures on Religions,* Count Nikolaus von Zinzendorf, founder of the Moravian missionary movement in 1727, describes such a spiritual wake-up call: "No man can create faith in himself. Something must happen to him which Luther calls 'the divine work in us' which changes us, gives us new birth, and makes us completely different people in heart, spirit, mind, and all our powers."[1] This personal spiritual awakening comes to the heart of every individual who meets Jesus Christ as Savior.

It was true for John Wesley, eventual founder of Methodism, in 1738 when he attended a Moravian gathering: "I went very unwillingly to a society in Aldersgate Street, where one was reading Luther's preface to the Epistle to the Romans. While he was describing the change which God makes in the heart through faith in Christ, I felt my heart strangely warmed. I felt I did trust in Christ, Christ alone for salvation; and an assurance was given me that He had taken away my sins, even mine, and saved me from the law of sin and death."[2]

John Wesley had met the Bright Morning Star (Revelation 22:16), the originator of all true spiritual awakening and the One who heralds (or proclaims) a genuine "new age"!

Knowing His Name

Several Greek words are combined to create the concept of Christ as the Bright Morning Star—the star that heralds the dawning of a new day (see Revelation 22:16).

Aster, the Greek word for *star* used in Revelation 22:16, is combined with the adjectives *bright* and *morning. Bright* indicates Christ's dominance, and *morning* denotes His newness or freshness. Jesus, like the morning star heralding the dawn, outshines the darkness and calls us to be expectant and refreshed.

Second, the Greek word *phosphoros,* from which we derive our word *phosphorus,* is translated "day star," yet another title of Christ found in 2 Peter 1:19 (KJV). It means "light-bearing," and was usually used to describe the planet Venus, which just before dawn often appears unusually bright on the eastern horizon.

Another Greek word—*phosphorion* (translated "window")—is derived from the same root word translated as "star." What a wonderful image—Jesus brings light to us in the same way that a window opens a room to the outside sunlight, which then illuminates the entire room. He is the Window of God, opening to us all of God's glowing freshness.

A third word, *anatole,* occurs in Luke 1:78. It is translated "Dayspring from on high" in the King James Version and "Sunrise" or "morning light" in other translations. As a whole, when Jesus refers to Himself as the Bright Morning Star, He is providing us with a threefold analysis of His nature. His brightness reveals the darkness of our sin or suffering which cannot prevail; His shining declares that a new day is at hand as we move into His light; and His radiance announces that His coming is at hand and we must be ready for that moment.

Living His Name

A missionary in Africa describes a unique tribal custom that he witnessed when traveling with a tribe. Every night, just before lying down to sleep, the tribesmen would say to one another,

Begin your day *by being "dipped in God" through a prayer encounter in Jesus' name!*

"Lutanda, lutanda"—their word for "morning star." Saying it before sleep was a reminder that they would be up and on their way before sunrise. The morning star's appearance would be their signal that dawn was coming soon and it was time to awaken.

How appropriate that Jesus' name, our Bright Morning Star, alerts our hearts to rise up, ready to bring a spirit of worship into our day. As we reflect God's nature and character in all we do, we are taking His light into the darkness we encounter, whether on the job, in school, or throughout our neighborhood. Jesus said, "You are the light of the world" (Matthew 5:14).

Praying His Name

Are you an early riser? "Early will I seek thee" is a phrase frequently found in the King James Bible (Psalm 63:1; Psalm 57:8; and Psalm 108:2, KJV). The phrase literally means, "From the very dawning of the day I will hunger after You." Even Jesus, who prayed "before daybreak the next morning," knew that early communion with His heavenly Father was valuable (Mark 1:35).

In a very practical sense, we could begin praying in Jesus' name, the Bright Morning Star ("He Who Heralds the Morning"), with a commitment to spend time with Christ early in the morning. There's no better way to awaken spiritual sensibilities than to immerse ourselves in the fullness of God. Describing such an awakening, D. H. Lawrence wrote in *Shadows,* "And if tonight my soul may find her peace in sleep, and sink in good oblivion, and in the morning wake like a new-opened flower, then I have been dipped again in God, and new-created."[3]

What a way to begin a day, by being "dipped in God" through a prayer encounter in Jesus' name! Oh, that we would heed Paul's "wake-up call": "Awake, O sleeper, rise up from the dead, and Christ will give you light" (Ephesians 5:14). Awaken to the bright beams of God's glory shining through His window on eternity! Awaken to the bright hope of a new day in the radiance of His presence. Awaken to this bright reminder: Jesus is coming again! Let these thoughts fill your prayers today in Jesus' name, the Bright Morning Star.

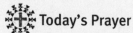 **Today's Prayer**

FATHER OF LIGHT, IN WHOM IS NO CHANGE OR SHADOW OR TURNING, I COME PRAYERFULLY TO YOU. I WANT TO LIVE AS A CHILD OF LIGHT—TO ELIMINATE ALL THE HIDDEN WORKS OF DARKNESS. I WANT TO BE A LIGHT FOR YOU WHEREVER I GO. AND SO I COME THIS DAY IN JESUS' NAME, THE BRIGHT MORNING STAR—WHO HERALDS THE DAWN OF THE ULTIMATE NEW DAY. MAY YOUR LIFE IN ME SHINE GLORIOUSLY. TODAY LET ME SO SHINE THAT PEOPLE WILL SEE YOUR LOVE AND LIFE IN ME AND KNOW THAT HOWEVER DARK IT SEEMS, YOU ARE THE POLE STAR OF MY LIFE. I RISE TO PRAISE YOU. COME SOON, LORD JESUS, THE SUN OF RIGHTEOUSNESS, TO RULE OVER ALL THIS EARTH. I LOVE YOU, LORD. IN YOUR NAME, AMEN.

MY PERSONAL MEDITATIONS

_____

_____

_____

_____

_____

_____

_____

_____

_____

MORE NAMES FOR JESUS

Check the index beginning on page 162 for these additional names for Jesus that suggest the Bright Morning Star: Morning Light; Morning Star; Star Rising from Jacob.

A Foundation Stone

Therefore, this is what the Sovereign LORD says: "Look! I am placing a foundation stone in Jerusalem, a firm and tested stone. It is a precious cornerstone that is safe to build on. Whoever believes need never be shaken.   *Isaiah 28:16*

Hollywood, California: It's a mecca for people frantically seeking success, fame, and fortune. Only a relative few have actually "made it"—commemorated by bronze star plaques embedded in a stretch of sidewalks along Hollywood Boulevard and Vine Street. The names of celebrities in the entertainment industry appear on this Walk of Fame. In the world's eyes, it appears that these men and women have mastered their destinies. Yet a closer look reveals plaques half-covered with debris, splattered with mud, or discolored with ground-in gum.

Contrast that image with what God promises His people: "I am placing a foundation stone in Jerusalem, a firm and tested stone. . . . a precious cornerstone that is safe to build on" (Isaiah 28:16). God lifts our lives out of this world's mire and places them on the solid ground of His purposes. His Word declares, "I waited patiently for the LORD to help me, and he turned to me and heard my cry. He lifted me out of the pit of despair, out of the mud and the mire. He set my feet on solid ground and steadied me as I walked along" (Psalm 40:1-2). And the reward of walking God's path doesn't only apply to this life. The prophet Daniel declared that the redeemed of the Lord—those whose lives are built upon the Foundation Stone laid by God—shall "shine like the stars forever" (Daniel 12:3).

Knowing His Name

What does calling God the "foundation stone" actually mean? In Isaiah 28, that name emphasizes God's commitment to provide stability to a culture immersed in uncertainty.

In this biblical account, we arrive during the reign of Ahaz, one of Judah's most wicked kings. At the height of his wickedness, Ahaz actually pillaged the Temple in Jerusalem, then barred the door from worship. Ahaz's behavior unleashed suffering and defeat upon Judah—once at the hands of Pekah the Syrian and later during a civil war against the northern kingdom of Israel. In the second conflict, Ahaz's son was killed and two hundred thousand women and children were taken captive (see 2 Chronicles 28).

Isaiah 28: 7, 13 describes a people "who reel with wine" and "stagger as they render decisions," and who will ultimately "stumble and fall . . . be injured, trapped, and captured," yet the prophet issues a contrasting promise. He explains that the Lord is committed to preparing the way for His chosen people to rise and stand solidly and securely amid the culture of the day. Through Isaiah the Lord declared, "Look! I am placing a foundation stone in Jerusalem, a firm and tested stone. It is a precious cornerstone that is safe to build on" (Isaiah 28:16). The heart of God's promise is this: No matter how uncertain the world may be, there is a solid place on which the followers of Jesus can stand. And that place is His name—a foundation stone.

Remarkably, God Himself pledges to lay this foundation—committing Himself to establish a place where life can be lived with stability and certainty. Talk about confidence for believers in Him! If God lays a foundation, it is certain that something is going to be built upon it. God is not in the habit of starting projects without finishing them. The Bible says, "God, who began the good work within you, will continue his work until it is finally finished on the day when Christ Jesus returns" (Philippians 1:6).

The remarkable thing about

*God is committed to **provide stability** to a culture immersed in uncertainty.*

this foundation is not only the promise for future development but also for future durability. The Hebrew word *yasad* found here was commonly used to describe the establishing of a foundation. But it also referred to rulers or counselors "sitting together" to confer on important matters. It suggests that careful consultation will insure stable planning, a truth emphasized by the writer of Proverbs who declares wisdom is secured by "many advisers" (Proverbs 11:14; 15:22). Can you see the depth of this foundation upon which we are to build our lives?

Living His Name

Today's world operates at a frantic pace: people grasping for more and more, stampeding to seize opportunities, rushing to buy the newest gadget. It's easy to be caught up in that mentality, to become urgent and desperate about life rather than confidently waiting for God's plan to unfold. It's important to remember God's pledge: "Look!" He says to us. "See what solid ground I have for you to build your life upon— for developing plans, making decisions, and working out problems. Look! It's sure footing, an established foundation. In my name you will find stability!"

Praying His Name

Stability is a foundational quality of the name of Jesus. To pray in Jesus' name is to approach His throne with unqualified assurance. It is to pray confidently as Thomas Aquinas did:

Give me, O Lord, a steadfast heart, which no unworthy affection may drag downwards; give me an unconquered heart, which no tribulation can wear out; give me an upright heart, which no unworthy purpose may tempt aside. Bestow on me also, O Lord my God, understanding to know You, diligence to seek You, wisdom to find You, and faithfulness that may finally embrace You, through Jesus Christ our Lord. Amen.[1]

Think of the areas in your life where you are most vulnerable. Each day ask the Lord to reveal possible temptations and pray that you will remain strong as you stand on His foundation. Pray as John Wesley did before embarking on a treacherous mission:

Fix Thou our steps, O Lord, that we stagger not at the world, but steadily go on to our glorious home. . . . The winds are often rough, and our own weight presses us downwards. Reach forth, O Lord, Thy saving hand, and speedily deliver us. Teach us, O Lord, to use this transitory life as pilgrims returning to their beloved *home; . . . that we take what our journey requires, and not think of settling in a foreign country.²*

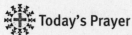 ## Today's Prayer

HOLY FATHER GOD, I WAIT QUIETLY BEFORE YOU. THE WORLD WANTS TO RUSH ME, SAYING IF I DON'T HURRY, I CAN'T GET AHEAD. BUT AS I PRAY IN JESUS' NAME, I TAKE MY PLACE UPON THE FOUNDATION STONE YOU HAVE LAID FOR MY LIFE IN HIM. I PRAYERFULLY AFFIRM—"MY HOPE IS BUILT ON NOTHING LESS!" DIRECT MY LIFE TODAY, DEAR LORD. LET ALL THAT I DO BE ENDURING BECAUSE YOU ARE LEADING ME EACH STEP OF THE WAY. IN THE NAME OF MY FOUNDATION—JESUS, YOUR SON, MY SAVIOR. AMEN!

MY PERSONAL MEDITATIONS

_____

_____

_____

_____

_____

_____

_____

_____

MORE NAMES FOR JESUS

Check the index beginning on page 162 for these additional names for Jesus that suggest a Foundation Stone: My Fortress; My Rock; My Rock of Protection; Strong Refuge.

A Refiner and Purifier

He will sit like a refiner of silver, burning away the dross. He will purify the
Levites, refining them like gold and silver, so that they may once again offer
acceptable sacrifices to the Lord.   Malachi 3:3

If you peruse certain aisles of any discount store, you'll conclude that most people want things to be clean—their clothes,
their kitchens and bathrooms, especially themselves! Although
the phrase, "Cleanliness is next to godliness" is not found in
Scripture, it is God's goal for everyone who trusts in Him to
experience spiritual purity and growth. He longs to cleanse us of
those spiritual "germs" that rob us of purity. That's why our faith
is sometimes "tested by fire" (1 Peter 1:7, NKJV).

In his *Sermons,* Phillips Brooks explains, "In what strange quarries
and stone-yards the stones for the celestial wall are being hewn!
Out of the hillsides of humiliated pride; deep in the darkness of
crushed despair; in the fretting and dusty atmosphere of little cares;
in the hard cruel contacts that man has with man; wherever souls
are being tried and ripened, in whatever commonplace and homely
ways—there God is hewing out the pillars for His temple."[1]

God continually draws us closer to His purifying fire so we
might be more like Him. If we're honest, we'd all have to admit
that our lives need continual purifying. Thomas à Kempis wrote
in *The Imitation of Christ,* "I have never found yet any religious
person so perfect that he had sometimes absenting of grace or
some diminishing of fervor; and there was never yet any saint so
highly rapt but that, first or last, he had some temptation. He is
not worthy to have the high gift of contemplation that hath not
suffered for God some tribulation."[2]

"All have sinned and come short of the glory of God" (Romans
3:23, KJV). Even after we've surrendered our lives to Christ,
we're still human. Does the message of this bumper sticker hit
home? "Lead me not into temptation. I can find it for myself!"
We need Jesus, our Refiner and Purifier, to cleanse us, purify us,
and help us grow.

Knowing His Name

The prophet Malachi, who refers to God as a Refiner and Purifier (Malachi 3:3), was addressing a self-centered group of complainers who had forgotten God's faithfulness. These Israelites were consumed with their own interests. They begrudgingly served the Lord. "It isn't really worth it to serve God," the people seemed to say (see Malachi 3:14). When the Lord challenged their indifference, the self-serving "saints" became indignant. In essence, they replied, "What are You talking about?" (see Malachi 1:6-8).

This scene reveals people who are accustomed to being around godliness, but refuse to grow up. Yet God's promise rings out: "The Lord . . . will suddenly come to his Temple" (Malachi 3:1). His visit will result in purging and purifying such as when a refiner works with precious metals. The prophecy proclaims, "He will be like a blazing fire that refines metal, or like a strong soap that bleaches clothes" (Malachi 3:2). God's desire is to refine their character as well as purify their lives.

Living His Name

Refiner and Purifier. Fire and soap. Let's look at these two images more closely, beginning with the one you encounter every day—soap.

When I think of strong soap, I immediately think of laundry soap. *The image of strong soap depicts the thorough process of cleaning.* You start the machine, put your clothes in the water, add soap, and wait for the presence of the soap to thoroughly penetrate and clean the clothes.

The same principle is at work when we allow the presence of Jesus to invade any uncleanness in us. At any time, on any day, He will readily cleanse it. It doesn't require special incantations or completing a self-improvement course. It is simply a matter of inviting Jesus into the unclean parts of our lives. You might feel ashamed to ask Him there. But He who left the excellence of heaven to condescend to the pollution of earth is not threatened by either the presence or power of sin. "The Spirit who lives in you is greater," the Bible says

Let God burn away the things which prevent
His glory from being reflected through you.

(1 John 4:4). If your mind, heart, habits, or actions are stunting your spiritual growth, invite Jesus into your failures, to make you clean to the core.

Second, *the image of a metal refiner depicts our Lord's gentleness.* The soap works with strength; the refiner works with sensitivity. Metal is refined by melting it down and removing the impurities or dross. As the metal is heated, the dross rises to the surface and the refiner carefully draws it off. If the temperature is too high, the metal will burn; if it's too low, not all the impurities will rise to the top. A skilled refiner is both sensitive and patient. He is sensitive to how much heat is needed for the process, and will patiently remove each impurity. The result is a mirrorlike quality to the surface of the molten metal that effectively reflects the face of the refiner himself.

Praying His Name

God's purifying power works continuously in our lives. But especially during prayer He reveals where we need to grow in our lives. When we pray in Jesus' name, our Refiner and Purifier, we become sensitive to the gentle "searchings" of the Holy Spirit, Who will draw out our secret sins. Poet Christina Rossetti spoke for all of us when she wrote:

As the wind is Thy symbol,
so forward our goings.

As the dove, so launch us
heavenwards.

As water, so purify our spirits.

As a cloud, so abate our temptations.

As dew, so revive our languor.

As fire, so purge out our dross.[3]

Have you ever felt like you're sitting on a celestial "hot seat" when you pray? It is our Refiner and Purifier pushing things to the surface that need to be removed, cleansed.

Don't be afraid to let God burn away the things which prevent His glory from being reflected through you. Pray for a new transparency in Jesus' name, our Refiner and Purifier. Echo the words of St. Augustine:

O Lord, the house of my soul is
narrow; enlarge it, that You may
enter in. It is ruinous, O repair it!
It displeases Your sight; I confess it,
I know. But who shall cleanse it, to
whom shall I cry out but to You?
Cleanse me from my secret faults,
O Lord, and spare Your servant
from strange sins.[4]

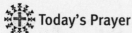

Today's Prayer

LORD JESUS CHRIST, I WANT YOU TO BE MY REFINER AND PURIFIER. I WANT YOU TO GROW ME! RIGHT NOW, I HAVE PLACES WHERE SIN INFESTS MY THOUGHTS, MY HABITS, MY LIFE. I ASK YOUR FORGIVENESS. I WANT YOUR PRESENCE TO WASH OVER ME LIKE CLEANSING SOAP. LAUNDER MY SOUL AND MY MIND TODAY.

AND LORD, WHEREVER YOUR REFINING FIRE NEEDS TO BE APPLIED, I WANT YOU TO BURN AWAY THE DROSS. TAKE OUT ANYTHING THAT CHEAPENS THE TREASURED QUALITY OF YOUR WORK IN ME. DEAR SAVIOR, DON'T STOP UNTIL YOUR IMAGE CAN BE SEEN. FOR I PRAY THIS IN YOUR NAME, MY REFINER AND PURIFIER. AMEN.

MY PERSONAL MEDITATIONS

_____

_____

_____

_____

_____

_____

_____

_____

_____

_____

MORE NAMES FOR JESUS

Check the index beginning on page 162 for these additional names for Jesus that suggest a Refiner and Purifier: Holy; Holy and Awe-Inspiring; Holy One; Jehovah-Mekaddishkem: The Lord Who Makes You Holy; Truly Righteous.

The One Who Holds My Head High

But you, O LORD, are a shield around me; you are my glory, the one who holds my head high. Psalm 3:3

How often do you find yourself using the excuse "I can't" when you're asked to do something? One of the first things a counselor often advises clients to eliminate from their vocabulary is the phrase "I can't." "I can't get along with my wife"; "I can't quit smoking"; "I can't control my temper"; "I can't hold down a job"; "I can't witness for Jesus." Any difficult task seems a prime candidate for the "I can't" list.

In Philippians 4:13, the apostle Paul destroys the "I can't" mentality in a single, all-encompassing confession: "For *I can* do everything through Christ, who gives me strength" (Philippians 4:13, italics added). Expanding on Paul's words, *The Amplified Bible* reads: "I have strength for all things in Christ Who empowers me [I am ready for anything and equal to anything through Him Who infuses inner strength into me; I am self-sufficient in Christ's sufficiency]" (4:13, AMP).

When Paul says we can do anything "through Christ," he is reminding us that our confidence and power is in Christ, Who lifts us above circumstances that could defeat us. The psalmist said it simply: "But you, O LORD, are . . . the one who holds my head high" (Psalm 3:3).

Knowing His Name

This psalm catapults you into the middle of a family drama. King David is running for his life from his son Absalom. As the king eludes his pursuer, he pictures the Lord as a "shield," "my glory," and the "one who holds my head high." The tone of the psalm moves from a desperate cry in the midst of trouble to confidence in the Lord's power for deliverance. It begins, "O Lord, I have so many enemies; so many are against me. So many are saying, "'God will never rescue him!'" (vv. 1-2), and ends with this confident assessment: "Victory comes from you, O LORD. May you bless your people" (v. 8). How can such confusion be transformed into such confidence? Because "you, O LORD, are . . . the one who holds my head high."

The word *head* used in this verse relates to a person's rights, authority, or position. David is essentially saying, "What and who I am is being assaulted." In fact, Absalom was trying to steal David's kingdom. (In chapters 15–18 of 2 Samuel, you can find the details of Absalom's treason against his father.) Remarkably, David refuses to assert his own authority to stop his son. Instead, he was determined to allow the Lord to defend him. David knew that the "one who holds my head high" doesn't forget His people when opposition arises.

Psalm 3 exalts the One who alone establishes authority, rights, and power. God alone is able to restore what man attacks or steals. We can be confident that no one can take away what God wants us to have. The Lord is the one who "holds up" (i.e., raises, elevates, exalts) our places, privileges, positions, or person.

Living His Name

Living today in Jesus' name, the One Who Holds My Head High, is beginning the day trusting that we will be saturated with Christ's confidence. God knows our weaknesses as well as our strengths. He can strengthen the weaknesses and maximize the strengths. It is His nature to "hold [us] up high."

By *God's grace* we can rid our vocabularies of every "I can't."

The Hebrew origin of the expression "holds up high" (Psalm 3:3) comes from the Hebrew word *ruhm*. The word is used in different ways throughout the Old Testament. In Ezra 9:9, it is used to describe the raising up or building of the Temple; in Ezekiel 31:4, it describes what happens to a plant when it is watered; in Psalm 27:5 and 18:19 it is placing someone in a safe place; and in Isaiah 1:2 it refers to the raising up of children. Look at how the Lord holds up concerns about our home, our work, our provision, our safety, and even the raising of our children. All of this results from learning to live in Jesus' name—the One Who Holds My Head High.

By God's grace we can rid our vocabularies of every "I can't." In *Stones and Bread* Gerald Vann wrote, "Trying to be perfect means trying to do your particular best, with the particular graces God has given you. You cannot pray like Saint Teresa any more than you can sing like Caruso, but how foolish if for that reason you give up trying to pray or sing at all. What God asks of you is that you should do your best, not Saint Teresa's best."[1]

Praying His Name

As you pray today anticipate each circumstance that might require special confidence. Is there a difficult task you'll face later on? Have you been struggling with depression, feeling as if you're caught in spiritual quicksand? Picture that difficult task or depressed spirit and visually imagine Christ coming to you and gently holding your head up with His tender touch. Can you feel Him holding you up even now? He not only holds your head up but lifts you confidently to your feet.

The enemy Satan will try to limit your effectiveness in prayer. No matter how enormous your problems are, remember that God is more powerful. Thankfully, circumstances become less devastating when you realize that Christ, the One Who Holds My Head High, is beside you. You can join in Tennyson's confident words from *In Memorium:*

And all is well, tho' faith and form
Be sunder'd in the night of fear;
Well roars the storm to those that hear
A deeper voice across the storm.[2]

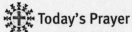 **Today's Prayer**

I AM MOVED TODAY, LORD, WHEN I THINK HOW COMPLETELY YOU WILL RESTORE EVERYTHING ONE DAY TO ITS ORIGINAL CREATED SPLENDOR. UNTIL THEN, MY HEAD IS OFTEN DOWNCAST, LORD: I'M ASHAMED OF MY SIN OR MY COWARDICE OR MY FOOLISHNESS; MY HEAD FALLS BECAUSE I LOSE CONFIDENCE OR HOPE OR FAITH THAT THINGS WILL WORK OUT. BUT TODAY, HOPE RISES. I'M REMINDED THAT YOU NOT ONLY LOVE, SAVE, FORGIVE, AND REDEEM, BUT YOU LEAN OVER TO TAKE ME IN YOUR ARMS. YOU STRETCH FORTH YOUR HANDS TO TAKE MY DESPAIRING SPIRIT AND YOU HOLD MY HEAD HIGH LIKE AN ASSURING FATHER, LIKE A COMFORTING MOTHER. MY HEART SAYS, AMEN, LORD, THANK YOU. IN JESUS' NAME, AMEN.

MY PERSONAL MEDITATIONS

_____

_____

_____

_____

_____

_____

_____

_____

_____

MORE NAMES FOR JESUS

Check the index beginning on page 162 for these additional names for Jesus that suggest the One Who Holds My Head High: My Helper, My Strength and My Song; One Who Rescues; Refuge to the Needy; Source of Hope.

The Radiance
of God's Glory

The Son radiates God's own glory and expresses the very character of God, and he sustains everything by the mighty power of his command. When he had cleansed us from our sins, he sat down in the place of honor at the right hand of the majestic God in heaven.   Hebrews 1:3

What is the brightest thing you can think of? The sun? A star? A planet? How about the Creator of the sun, the stars, and the planets?

At one point in his book *Imitation of Christ*, Thomas à Kempis offered this prayer, "O everlasting Light, surpassing all created luminaries, flash forth Thy lightning from above, piercing all the most inward parts of my heart. Make clean, make glad, make bright, and make alive my spirit, with all the powers thereof, that I may cleave unto Thee in ecstasies of joy."[1]

Jesus, alone, is the radiance of the glory of the Lord. He is the reflection of God's immeasurable excellence. And everywhere we look we see this glory. As Henry Ward Beecher wrote, "Nature would be scarcely worth a puff of the empty wind if it were not that all nature is but a temple, of which God is the brightness and the glory."[2]

Knowing His Name

Glory refers to that which exceeds or excels. A craftsman's glory is his ability to use the ordinary to create the extraordinary. An athlete's glory is using his skills to seize the moment and deliver the home run, touchdown, or goal, or to cross the finish line a stride ahead of the field.

We all harbor dreams of glory. For most of us, the realities of life and our own limitations change our dreams. But Christ has come to bring every one of us into His glory. He wants to give us the capacity to obtain what seems unapproachable and unattainable (Hebrews 2:10). In Jesus' name, the Radiance of God's Glory, we can experience and know *real* glory!

Do you strive for excellence in everything you do? It seems that many people strive for mediocrity, or at least are satisfied with "getting by" with less than the finest effort. That is contrary to Christ. He wants His excellence to shine through us until everything that is unworthy of His presence is crowded out.

It's true that daily pressures often result in second-rate performances. Yet, the Bible tells us that Christ "in us" affords the "assurance of sharing his glory" (Colossians 1:27). This promise not only refers to an eternal future in the glory of His presence, but to the glory of Christ working His splendor in and through us right here, right now.

The writer to the Hebrews states that Christ Himself expresses the very character of God (Hebrews 1:3). Or, as Paul suggests, we haven't seen "the glory of God that is seen in the face of Jesus Christ" (2 Corinthians 4:6). In the person of Jesus we have been presented with the ultimate of God's excellence. Christ is the best. He cannot be excelled. He is a complete picture of excellence, of all that man can hope to become. And when we allow Christ to live in us, we can become the finest we can be in Him.

Christ wants to give us the capacity to obtain what seems unapproachable and unattainable.

Day 7 {EXCELLENCE}

Living His Name

Let's be honest: Being excellent at anything takes hard work. It can take a toll physically, emotionally, and mentally. Achieving excellence can be plagued with perfectionism, criticism, and competition. God has a more excellent way which is restful, filled with His grace, goodness, and mercy. But to experience His radiant glory is a three-part process.

First, *we are called to expect Christ's excellence*. In 2 Corinthians 3, the apostle Paul makes a comparison between how God's mighty power was demonstrated in the Old Testament (Moses' face was set aglow by it) and how the release of the Holy Spirit demonstrates "the overwhelming glory of the new way" in the New Testament (v. 10). Verse 18, the climax of this passage, lays out the promise that we can expect will be fulfilled: "And the Lord—who is the Spirit—makes us more and more like him as we are changed into his glorious image."

Second, *we are called to approach Christ's excellence*. The overwhelming radiance of God's throne is described vividly by John in Revelation 4:5. In the first chapter of Revelation, the radiance of Christ Himself is described in great detail. Studying these fascinating details and noting John's response as he falls before such majesty helps us capture a sense of what is meant by Paul's description of Christ in 1 Timothy 6:15-16:

For at just the right time Christ will be revealed from heaven by the blessed and only almighty God, the King of all kings and Lord of all lords. He alone can never die, and he lives in light so brilliant that no human can approach him. No human eye has ever seen him, nor ever will. All honor and power to him forever! Amen.

The unapproachableness of such excellence and glory would intimidate us in our quest except for one fact: God's grace has opened the door for our approach! Unredeemed man at his best can never become worthy of approach. But the radiance of God's glorious excellence displayed to us in Jesus Christ has not only manifested that glory but has made a way for us to enter into it! The psalmist said, "What joy for those you choose to bring near, those who live in your holy courts. What festivities await us inside your holy Temple" (Psalm 65:4).

Finally, *we are called to witness and experience Christ's excellence*. No episode in the Bible is more stirring than Isaiah's description of the glory of God in the Temple (Isaiah 6:1-8). Here the prophet outlines a complete message on the awesomeness, the awareness, and the action of God's excellence. In Isaiah's experience we discover a road map just waiting to lead us to the glory of the Lord. If we follow it in prayer, we too can experience the working of Christ's excellence.

Praying His Name

Using Isaiah's experience, a threefold outline emerges to help us pray in Jesus' name, the Radiance of God's Glory.

First, *come with worship and behold the awesomeness of God.* "I saw the Lord. He was sitting on a lofty throne, and the train of his robe filled the Temple," declared the prophet (Isaiah 6:1). There is a difference between the pursuit of excellence from a human perspective and a divine perspective. The former strives to put forth the best human effort; the divine approach to excellence begins with bowing before the Lord.

The full meaning of the

Hebrew word *ra-ah,* translated "saw" in this verse, is significant. It means to see something with absolute clarity. To worship God effectively we must have a proper view of Him, not allowing anything to obstruct our vision. That divinely focused view only comes to those who study God's nature and character as revealed in His Word. Anyone who plunges deeply into God's Word rises highest in their praises of His glory.

Second, *open your heart to the fire of God's purifying promise.* "I am doomed, for I am a sinful man. I have filthy lips, and I live among a people with filthy lips," the prophet prayed (Isaiah 6:5). Isaiah was honest about who he was; the path to excellence is paved with self-honesty, not pretension. Paul stressed how important confession of sin is: "Let us cleanse ourselves from everything that can defile our body or spirit. And let us work toward complete holiness because we fear God" (2 Corinthians 7:1).

Finally, *allow God's work to mature you and prepare you for service.* Isaiah invited the cleansing fire of God into his life, then immediately offered himself for whatever task God had for him to do. "Here I am. Send me," he cries (Isaiah 6:8). God may well have a specific mission with your name on it. As you saturate yourself in the Radiance of God's Glory, the person of Christ Himself, listen for what He has planned for you.

Make a habit of applying divine "excellence" to all that you do. Realizing that Jesus is the Radiance of God's Glory and praying in Jesus' name opens the way to living in the splendid fullness of all that His person implies.

Today's Prayer

DEAR LORD, THERE SEEM TO BE SO MANY TIMES I AM SWALLOWED UP BY THE DISCOURAGING SENSE OF BEING SECOND RATE. I TRY SO HARD AND DO SO POORLY. I START SO WELL AND END SO QUICKLY. I GIVE IT MY BEST AND DISCOVER IT ISN'T ENOUGH. AND SO I COME TO YOU, THE SAVIOR OF MY SOUL—YOU WHO HAVE SO COMPLETELY SAVED ME THAT NOTHING OF MY OWN FAILURE OR SIN COULD RESTRICT THE UNLIMITED POWER OF YOUR SALVATION.

COME TO ME NOW. COME IN THE EXCELLENCY OF YOUR GLORIOUS PERSON AND FILL MY LIFE. AT THOSE POINTS WHERE MY OWN SHORTCOMINGS PREVAIL, COME IN THE EXCELLENCE OF YOUR NATURE AND POWER. I CHOOSE YOU TODAY. I RECEIVE YOUR EXCELLENCE AS MY RESOURCE, MY SUPPLY, AND MY SHELTER. I BOTH RECEIVE AND TAKE REFUGE IN YOUR COMPLETENESS.

THANK YOU, JESUS. MY TODAYS CAN'T BE MEDIOCRE ANYMORE. YOUR EXCELLENCE IS BEGINNING TO OVERFLOW AROUND ME. AMEN.

MY PERSONAL MEDITATIONS

_____
_____
_____
_____
_____
_____
_____
_____
_____
_____
_____
_____
_____
_____

MORE NAMES FOR JESUS

Check the index beginning on page 162 for these additional names for Jesus that suggest the Radiance of God's Glory: Assurance of Glory; Glory of Your People Israel; God Who Gives Me Life.

The Hidden Manna

Anyone with ears to hear must listen to the Spirit and understand what he is saying to the churches. To everyone who is victorious I will give some of the manna that has been hidden away in heaven. And I will give to each one a white stone, and on the stone will be engraved a new name that no one understands except the one who receives it.   Revelation 2:17

Have you ever experienced real hunger?

With college bills piling up and no employment, a young couple sat down to eat a meager meal of a single hamburger patty and a glass of milk each. The young husband offered thanks and a simple petition: "Lord, we're not asking for much, just enough to get by." With tears in his eyes he added, "At least, Lord, give us the staples we need to go with what little we have. That's all we ask for Lord, just the staples!"

As they began to eat, the husband winced with sudden pain. Something sharp was in the meat. Fishing the object from his mouth, he stared in amazement at a small metal staple. Both husband and wife began laughing as the husband said aloud, "That's not what I meant, Lord!"

Rather than risk possible injury, the husband promptly headed back to the market with the uneaten meat. The store manager was deeply concerned, and, although the young husband didn't threaten legal action, the manager immediately sought to make amends. "Sir," the manager blurted out, "if you'll be so kind as to forget this ever happened, you can fill up one of those shopping carts with all the groceries you can use for a week. They're on the house!"

Knowing His Name

Take a moment to look around you right now. Wherever you are, I'm certain you see evidence of God's promise to provide. Maybe you're in your home surrounded by furniture, clothing, and the like. Or you're sitting outside surrounded by beautiful trees, flowers, and birds. These details of life we often take for granted are blessings God designed specifically for His children. Henry Ward Beecher observed, "So many are God's kindnesses to us that, as drops of water, they run together, and it is not until we are born up by the multitude of them, as by streams in deep channels, that we recognize them as coming from Him."[1]

What about the *hidden* provisions of God? The air we breathe, the lungs that take in the air, and the ability of the body to use that air to sustain life are all gracious gifts from God. His provisions are abundant and infinite, including the ultimate blessing of all: His very presence. Alfred Lord Tennyson said poetically in *The Higher Pantheism:*

Speak to Him, thou, for He hears, and Spirit with Spirit can meet—
Closer is He than breathing, and nearer than hands and feet.

Christ's presence clearly provides all we need—our Hidden Manna for surviving life's journey. In Revelation 2:17, Christ says, "To everyone who is victorious I will give some of the manna that has been hidden away in heaven." The manna Jesus is referring to is Himself. In John 6:31-35, Christ describes Himself as the Bread (Manna) who comes down from heaven, the final fulfillment of God's provision for His people.

The first mention of manna in the Old Testament occurs in Exodus 16:31, when God begins a forty-year-long miracle of provision for the Israelites. In Joshua 5:11-12, the manna disappears—"it was never seen again"—because the Israelites

Living today in Christ is recognizing that He, alone, is our secret provision *for all we need.*

were able to provide for themselves from crops they planted.

Now consider Revelation 2:12-17, the context in which the title "Hidden Manna" is included. Christ is writing to the church of Pergamum, praising them for their loyalty, but pointing out the sin in their midst. The church's impurity came from eating "food offered to idols" (v. 14). In other words, they were guilty of a worldly diet that led to excessive indulgence in other aspects of life.

What's the lesson for us? When we depend on human resources for our provision, or worse yet, compromise our faith to insure our personal or financial security, we open the door to ever-increasing failure. Christ wants us to depend on Him, and only Him, for sufficiency. The Father's guarantee of provision is to be our only grounds for security, whether material or physical.

Let's look again at Exodus 16. God commanded Moses to place a jar of manna in the Ark of the Covenant "to preserve it for all future generations" (Exodus 16:32-34). Despite intensive searches—by archaeologists and adventurers—the Ark of the Covenant with its contents is still lost

to history. Surely God removed it in order for us to focus on the One who is the true fulfillment of all the Ark represented—Christ Himself. "In Christ" we have the fulfillment of provision, of the manna that was sealed away until a future day.

Living His Name

Living today in Christ, our Hidden Manna, is recognizing that He, alone, is our "secret provision" for all we need. The Israelites' miracle supply of manna appeared mysteriously. The manna always arrived during the night when everyone was asleep.

Think of your own needs. Perhaps when God says, "I'll provide for you," He expects us to rest and let Him take care of the providing. Don't be too surprised if His provisions come when things seem to be at their darkest. Take heart, for God is already at work preparing tomorrow's provision today!

Praying His Name

To pray today in Jesus' name, our Hidden Manna, is to pray knowing that Christ is capable of providing our every need. It is to trust that there will be a continual and sufficient portion given by the King Himself at a "daily rate" for our entire lives. It is to pray confidently "Give us this day our daily bread."

Ignatius Loyola was the youngest of eleven children. He grew up in Spain centuries ago and he surely understood Christ to be the Hidden Manna. In 1534 when Loyola was forty-three years old, he surrendered all of his wealth and worldly claims. Loyola moved to Paris and gathered six disciples to establish a new order called "The Company of Jesus," or Jesuits. Twenty-two years later at Loyola's death, those half-dozen disciples had grown to one thousand, many of whom had gone to the ends of the earth as foreign missionaries. Ignatius Loyola trusted God implicitly. As he neared life's end, Loyola prayed with passion:

Take, Lord, all my liberty,
my memory, my understanding,
and my whole being.

You have given me all that I have,
all that I am, and I surrender all to
Your divine will, that You dispose
of me.

Give me only Your love and Your
grace, with this I am rich enough,
and I have no more to ask.[2]

 Today's Prayer

BREAD OF HEAVEN, SENT TO EARTH BELOW TO FILL THE STARVING HEART OF MAN 'MIDST THE FAMINE OF THIS WORLDLY SCENE; THOU ART WELCOME TO MY SOUL. BREAD OF HEAVEN, BROKEN ONCE FOR ALL, THAT NONE MUST GO UNFED TODAY. BROKEN MANNA GIVEN TO WEARY SOULS, COME, O MAN, AND FREELY DINE.

BREAD OF HEAVEN, BLEST REDEEMER, I'LL FEAST ON THY PROVISION; I'LL WALK AND NEVER LANGUISH, HAVING FED ON THY SUPPLY.

BREAD OF HEAVEN, SOON-RETURNING LORD, I'LL WATCH FOR HEAVEN'S RENDING, BUT UNTIL THEN I WILL BE STRENGTHENED BY THY LIFE WITHIN ME.

BREAD OF HEAVEN, JESUS CHRIST MY LORD, THOU ART MY SOUL'S SUPPLY. COME AND FEED ME, BLESSED SAVIOR, COME AND FILL ME. THOU HAST PROMISED TO SATISFY MY HUNGRY SOUL. AMEN.

Day **8** {PROVISION}

MY PERSONAL MEDITATIONS

_____
_____
_____
_____
_____
_____
_____
_____
_____
_____
_____
_____
_____
_____
_____
_____
_____
_____

_____

_____

_____

_____

_____

_____

_____

_____

_____

_____

_____

MORE NAMES FOR JESUS

Check the index beginning on page 162 for these additional names for Jesus that suggest the Hidden Manna: Bread of God; Bread of Life; Gift God Has for You; Jehovah-Jireh: The Lord Will Provide; Kernel of Wheat; True Bread from Heaven.

The Bridegroom

But while they were gone to buy oil, the bridegroom came. Then those who were ready went in with him to the marriage feast, and the door was locked.

Matthew 25:10

What happens to a bridegroom in that moment when he sees the love of his life coming down the aisle? He experiences a rush of affection for one person—his chosen bride. The same is true of God, our Bridegroom, whose affection for us is immeasurable.

"In the very beginning," wrote Charles Spurgeon in his *Sermons,* "when this great universe lay in the mind of God, like unborn forests in the acorn cup; long before the echoes waked the solitudes, before the mountains were brought forth, and long before the light flashed through the sky, God loved its chosen creatures."[1]

Gerhard Tersteegen in *On Inward Prayer* adds, "This spirit of ours does not belong to this world, nor to temporal objects; it was created for God alone and therefore is capable of enjoying true fellowship with Him. It may be, and it ought to be, His temple and sacred residence. Its occupation is to contemplate, love, and enjoy this beneficent Being, and to repose in Him; for this end it was created."[2]

Knowing His Name

Affection is at the heart of God, and at the heart of God's affection is the word *redemption*. Redemption, Christ's act of purchasing our salvation on the Cross, is an outflow of God's infinite love and affection for man. This was revealed in His desire to find a bride for His Son, Jesus Christ. It is in this context that we look to Jesus, the Bridegroom (Matthew 25:10).

Christ, the Bridegroom, appears in the parable of the ten bridesmaids where He instructs His followers to be prepared for His return. Not only does this parable illustrate the need for preparation but it gives a tender portrayal of Christ's relationship with us.

First, *Christ is the Savior Who gave Himself for our redemption* (Ephesians 5:23, 25). In laying down His life, our Lord has indicated not only the cost He was willing to pay for our salvation but how much we are worth to Him. Christ's love for us was so great that the cost (His life) was worth it to Him.

Second, *Christ is our Sanctifier who is patiently working with us to separate us completely unto Himself—and win us fully to Him* (Ephesians 5:26). How does this work? Ephesians 5:26 suggests that the washing of water by the Word is something Christ does as our heavenly Bridegroom. He patiently and tenderly takes all of His promises and uses them to cleanse our wounds, heal our bruises, and remove our stains. He is a tender Redeemer loving us into wholeness and purity.

Third, *Christ is our Nourisher who holds us close to feed and strengthen us*. The words *feeds* and *cares for* in this text (Ephesians 5:29) are words used to depict a nurse with a child. How powerfully this illustrates the affectionate way in which Christ protects us, answers each distressing call, and delights in drawing us near to feed and strengthen us.

Affection is at the heart of God, and at the heart of God's affection is the word redemption.

Living His Name

To live today in Jesus' name, our Bridegroom, is to renew our romance with Christ. Take time to fellowship lovingly with the Lord. Romance demands attention, and attention cultivates affection.

The most exciting event for Christ the Bridegroom is yet to come—when He returns for His bride. His affection for us culminates in His desire to be with us: "When everything is ready, I will come and get you, so that you will always be with me where I am" (John 14:3). That anticipated union should be an impetus to live a pure life, just as a bride keeps herself pure for her husband-to-be. John said, "But we do know that we will be like him, for we will see him as he really is. And all who have this eager expectation will keep themselves pure, just as he is pure" (1 John 3:2-3). Alfred Lord Tennyson described this anticipation:

> He lifts me to the golden doors,
> The flashes come and go;
> All heaven bursts her starry floors,
> And strews her light below,
> And deepens on and up! The gates
> Roll back, and far within

> For me the Heavenly
> Bridegroom waits,
> To make me pure of sin.
> The Sabbaths of Eternity!
> One Sabbath deep and wide—
> a light upon the shining sea—
> the Bridegroom and the Bride.³

Praying His Name

As we pray today in Jesus' name, our Bridegroom, set aside time just to love Him. Petitions sometimes clutter prayer. Requests are fine, but they can wait until after worship. For now just reach out and hold the hands of Jesus. Like the bride on her wedding night who longs only to be held by her bridegroom and lover, may we desire only to be held tightly in the arms of Christ. Worship Him. Exalt Him. Yearn for Him. Hunger after Christ alone.

England's Thomas More, the sixteenth-century scholar and lawyer who died for his religious convictions, learned to cultivate this desire for Christ. It was More's brilliant gifts that led him to various "cabinet" positions under King Henry VIII, most notably Lord Chancellor. When Henry VIII decided to divorce Katherine of Aragon, More opposed him. Later,

More resigned his chancellorship and was accused of treason when he refused to accept the oath declaring the king's papal supremacy. More's final words before being beheaded were, "The king's good servant, but God's first."

Thomas More lived out a prayer that he wrote earlier in his life:

Give me, good Lord, a longing to be with You, not to avoid the calamities of this world, nor so much to attain the joys of Heaven, as simply for love of You. And give me, good Lord, Your love and favor, which my love of You, however great it might be, could not deserve were it not for Your great goodness. These things, good Lord, that I pray for, give me Your grace to labor for.[4]

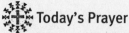

Today's Prayer

DEAR GOD, I COME BEFORE YOU LIKE ISAIAH, WHO LONG AGO SAID, "I LIVE WITH PEOPLE OF UNCLEAN LIPS AND I AM THAT WAY TOO." THERE IS SO MUCH POLLUTION IN MY WORLD, FATHER, IT SEEMS THAT LIVING A PURE LIFE IS IMPOSSIBLE. BUT I COME TO BE EMBRACED BY A LOVE SO PURE AND POWERFUL, SO COMFORTING AND SECURE, THAT THE WORLD CANNOT REDUCE ITS WORTH OR POLLUTE ITS PRECIOUSNESS.

IN THE NAME OF JESUS, THE HEAVENLY BRIDEGROOM, I WANT TO BE CAUGHT UP IN THE ARMS OF ETERNAL LOVE AND PURIFYING FIRE. BY YOUR FAITHFULNESS, JESUS, KEEP ME FAITHFUL. BY YOUR HOLINESS, SAVIOR, MAKE ME HOLY. BY YOUR LOVING-KINDNESS, LORD, MAKE THE LOVE I EXTEND TO OTHERS BE LIKE A BRIDEGROOM'S— BOTH LOVING AND KIND.

I ANTICIPATE THE DAY OF YOUR COMING AGAIN, LORD JESUS. BUT UNTIL THEN, WHILE I AM IN THE MIDST OF THESE DAYS SO INFECTED WITH SIN AND SINNING, I CHOOSE TO LIVE IN THE PROVISIONS OF YOUR NAME. TODAY, IN THE NAME OF THE BRIDEGROOM, I LIVE WITH HOPE AND HOLINESS. BY YOUR GREAT LOVE AND POWER AND IN YOUR NAME. AMEN.

Day 9 {AFFECTION}

MY PERSONAL MEDITATIONS

_____

_____

_____

_____

_____

_____

_____

_____

_____

_____

_____

_____

_____

_____

_____

_____

_____

_____

_____

_____

_____

_____

_____

_____

_____

_____

_____

_____

_____

MORE NAMES FOR JESUS

Check the index beginning on page 162 for these additional names for Jesus that suggest the Bridegroom: Desirable in Every Way; God of Compassion and Mercy; Love; My Beloved; My Lover.

✝ Day **10** {LIBERATION}

The Rescuer

And so all Israel will be saved. As the Scriptures say, "The one who rescues will come from Jerusalem, and he will turn Israel away from ungodliness."

Romans 11:26

What comes to mind when you hear the word *rescuer*? Have you ever been rescued from a life-threatening situation? If you're a believer in Christ, the answer is an emphatic yes!

A Welsh preacher began his morning sermon: "Friends, I have a question to ask. I cannot answer it. You cannot answer it. If an angel from heaven were here, he could not answer it. If a devil from hell were here, he could not answer it."

The entire congregation waited anxiously for the preacher's next words. After a longer than usual pause, he said, "The question is: 'How shall we escape if we neglect so great a salvation?'" (Hebrews 2:3, NKJV).

Jesus is our Rescuer, so neglecting Christ as Savior is neglecting our only hope of liberation. It is Christ the Rescuer who liberates us from sin's hold and brings us to a full realization of the power of God's holiness.

Knowing His Name

Paul introduces us to Christ the Rescuer in Romans 11:26 by referencing Psalm 14:7. The psalmist is assuring the believer that no matter how harsh the enemy's attack, the Lord will deliver us. In Isaiah 59:20 the title "Redeemer" reinforces God's covenant agreement that says once we become His, He will become our Rescuer (or Redeemer) and will "take away" our sins.

Let's look at some aspects of our Rescuer's work.

First, *Christ rescues us from "this life . . . dominated by sin and death"* (Romans 7:24).

Second, *Christ rescues us from our enemies* (Luke 1:74).

Third, *Christ rescues us from "certain death"* (2 Timothy 4:17). Here Jesus is pictured as our New Testament equivalent to Daniel's deliverer. Our adversary roars about as a lion seeking whom he may devour, but in Christ we have a Deliverer. We recall how Daniel seemed beyond hope in the lions' den, yet King Darius, who put him there in the first place, repeatedly affirmed that the Lord would be Daniel's deliverer (see Daniel 6:16, 20-27).

Finally, *Christ will rescue us from "the terrors of the coming judgment"* as Paul instructed the Thessalonians (1 Thessalonians 1:10). In Jesus' name we are confident in the hope that Christ's coming and His catching us away before earth's darkest hour will mark our ultimate deliverance in Him as our Rescuer.

The Greek word *rumoai,* used in these passages means "to rescue, save, deliver, preserve, or liberate." In *The Odyssey,* Homer uses the same word in referring to Odysseus's inability to save (*rumoai*) any of his men who, in the eyes of their various gods, were guilty and beyond salvation. Similarly, the gods themselves were unable to save (*rumoai*) any human being beyond the limits of his own destiny. But, hallelujah, in Christ we have a Rescuer who can save us in spite of our guilt. He is a God

Confront each temptation, remembering you're not alone— Jesus is beside you.

who brings us into an exciting new destiny through the deliverance that Christ alone can bring. Paul wrote, "This means that anyone who belongs to Christ has become a new person. The old life is gone; a new life has begun!" (2 Corinthians 5:17). We have a new destiny!

There are several definitions for the word *deliver*:

- to set free or save from evil or danger;
- to assist a woman at the birth of an offspring;
- to give forth or express in words, as in delivering a speech or announcement;
- to give, hand over, transfer, or carry to and leave at the proper place or places;
- to give or send forth (such as an oil well delivers twenty barrels a day);
- to strike a blow, as in "delivering a punch."

These definitions give a deeper understanding of the many ways Christ serves as our Rescuer. They also help us better appreciate the beautiful hymn:

*'Tis the grandest theme through
the ages rung,*

*'Tis the grandest theme for
a mortal tongue,*
*'Tis the grandest theme that the
world e'er sung,*
Our God is able to deliver thee![1]

Living His Name

To live today in Jesus' name, our Rescuer, is to approach each circumstance in the liberating power of Christ's presence. What is there in you that needs to be liberated today? Are you angry most of the time? Are your thoughts less than honoring to God? Have you become so dishonest that you can't recognize it anymore?

Picture yourself confronting each temptation, each sin, one at a time. Remember you're not alone—Jesus is beside you in each battle.

Your rescue is a multifaceted, never-ending work of Christ. The Bible tells us Christ "did rescue us from mortal danger, and he will rescue us again. We have placed our confidence in him, and he will continue to rescue us" (2 Corinthians 1:10). It's true that the instant we're saved, we all receive deliverance from sin's past penalty. As we grow in Christ, we can see how He continually rescues us from the power of present sin. And ultimately there will be rescue from sin's future when we meet Christ face-to-face. Hallelujah! Our rescue is complete: past, present, and future.

Praying His Name

As you pray today in Jesus' name, your Rescuer, pray through these aspects of rescuing deliverance: First, *deliver means to set free or save from evil or danger*. Can you think of a friend or loved one facing evil or in a dangerous circumstance where "freedom" or "deliverance" is needed? Ask for deliverance in that situation in Jesus' name.

Second, *deliver means to assist a woman in childbirth*. Is there something God has promised to "birth" or bring into existence in or through your life that is not yet a reality? Could this be God's time to deliver on that promise? You may wish to ask Him to help you "push forth" that dream into reality.

Third, *deliver means to give forth or express in words, as in deliv-ering a speech*. Is it time to talk to your boss, family member, or friend about Christ's love? Claim His empowerment to say the right thing.

Fourth, *deliver means to give, hand over, or transfer, as in delivering a message*. Maybe God wants to use you to deliver His special encouragement to one of His children struggling with discouragement.

Fifth, *deliver means to send forth, such as a well delivers oil or water*. In the world of business, someone who really "delivers" is a person who is hardwork-ing. God wants His children to "deliver" in everything they do. "Whatever you do, do well" (Ecclesiastes 9:10).

Finally, *deliver means to strike a blow such as "delivering a punch."* Armed with God's Word and praying in Jesus' name, send some blows in Satan's direction. As you do, remember: He who praises most swings best! Nothing seems to anger Satan more than a believer's worship of the Most High God.

Today's Prayer

DEAR LORD, I PRAY AS YOU TAUGHT ME, "DELIVER ME FROM EVIL." I PRAY AS DAVID PRAYED, "SEARCH ME AND KNOW ME AND SEE IF THERE BE SOME WICKED WAY IN ME, AND LEAD ME IN THE WAY EVERLASTING." I PRAY THAT YOU WOULD BREAK THE YOKE OF ANYTHING OTHER THAN YOUR SOUL-YOKE, WHICH MAKES ME YOUR DISCIPLE, YOUR SERVANT, AND YOUR FRIEND. LET YOUR HOLY SPIRIT BREAK MY BONDS AND SET MY SPIRIT FREE TO SERVE YOUR HOLY PURPOSE AND WORSHIP YOUR HOLY NAME— MY RESCUER, MIGHTY JESUS! IN YOUR NAME, AMEN.

MY PERSONAL MEDITATIONS

_____

_____

_____

_____

_____

_____

_____

_____

_____

_____

_____

_____

_____

_____

_____

_____

_____

_____

_____

_____

_____

_____

_____

MORE NAMES FOR JESUS

Check the index beginning on page 162 for these additional names for Jesus that suggest the Rescuer: Giver of Victory; Messenger of the Covenant; Personal Rescuer; Redeemer; Savior of the World.

11 {FORGIVENESS}

The Sacrifice That Atones for Our Sins

He himself is the sacrifice that atones for our sins—and not only our sins but the sins of all the world. 1 John 2:2

"If we really want to love we must learn how to forgive," wrote Mother Teresa. How loving are you today?

A story is told of an old woman who fell down the stairs as she was leaving a police station in Boston. She was taken by ambulance to a nearby hospital where she was in critical condition.

The nurse on duty befriended the woman and began to hear her story. "I have traveled all the way from California by myself, stopping at every major city between San Francisco and Boston," the woman said with tears in her eyes. "In each city I visit the police station and the hospital. My boy ran away from home and I have no idea where he is. I've got to find him. I've sold everything to make this journey, hoping for a miracle."

A ray of hope flashed in her eyes as she added, "He may come into this very hospital someday, and if he does, please promise you'll tell him that his two best friends never gave up on him."

Bending over the dying mother, the nurse whispered softly, "Tell me the names of those two friends so I can tell your son."

With trembling lips the mother replied, "Tell him those friends were God and his mother," and she closed her eyes and died.

God, even more than a forgiving mother, never gives up on one of His children. His forgiveness is uniquely infinite—both one of a kind and never ending. Who else in the universe can genuinely forgive and at the same time forget? (See Hebrews 8:12.) Since God is the quintessence of forgiveness, to think on God is to immerse oneself in thoughts of forgiveness rather than failure. As Søren Kierkegaard wrote, "When the thought of God does not remind a man of his sin but that he is forgiven, and the past is no longer the memory of how much he did wrong but of how much he was forgiven—then that man rests in the forgiveness of his sins."[1]

Knowing His Name

The apostle John elaborates on God's capacity to cover our sins (and thus forget them) by referring to Christ as the Sacrifice That Atones for Our Sins (1 John 2:2). In other, older Bible versions, the word *propitiation* is used for the phrase "sacrifice that atones." The New Testament Greek word *hilasterion* means "that which expiates, atones, or returns a favor." It was used in the ancient world of "votive offerings" (offerings given to fulfill certain vows of dedication). When used in reference to Christ it means our Lord unconditionally fulfilled His vow to provide the way for us to come back to God. Further, Jesus unconditionally fulfilled any perceived obligation on our part necessary for us to gain acceptance before God.

Many people make the mistake of thinking it is necessary to negotiate with God in order to be accepted by Him. They sometimes pray, "Lord, I'll do this for You if You'll do that for me." But as the Sacrifice That Atones for Our Sins, Christ has done *everything* necessary to "better

Because of Jesus' sacrifice, we can come to God knowing we are forgiven by Him.

us" in God's eyes. We can come to God freely, knowing we are forgiven by Him fully. What a joyous reality!

Interestingly, the same Greek word *hilasterion* is translated in Hebrews 9:5 as "the place of atonement." "The place of atonement" refers to the cover or lid placed on the Ark of the Covenant in the Holy of Holies. Even the Septuagint translation of the Old Testament, which was the Hebrew translated into the Greek, uses the word *hilasterion* when referring to the "atonement cover" in the Tabernacle (see Exodus 25:22).

On the Day of Atonement, the blood of the sacrificial lamb was poured on the *hilasterion* in the Holy of Holies by the high priest to atone for the people's sin. Inside the Ark of the Covenant, lay God's Law (the Ten Commandments) that man had broken. But now the atoning blood of a blameless substitute is placed between God and His broken law.

What a powerful picture of Christ. As our sinless substitute Jesus poured out His life on the cross as an atoning sacrifice before God. He comes between God's requirements for perfection and purity and our imperfection and impurity. Since Jesus is absolutely

perfect, God sees His sinless life instead of our sins and accepts us completely. We are "seated" in Christ (Ephesians 2:6), and receive God's mercy and forgiveness.

Living His Name
On the battlefield, a soldier cries "Cover me!" He's asking his comrades to provide artillery while he advances against the enemy. So Jesus "covers" us as we face daily spiritual warfare. Not only does He attack the enemy, but His blood covers all our sins and failures.

To live today in Jesus' name is not only to recognize Christ as the Sacrifice That Atones for Our Sins, but to take that spirit of loving forgiveness into our relationships with others. Just as Jesus covers and cleanses our sins with His blood (1 John 1:9), we need to cover the failures of others with our love (Proverbs 10:12, NKJV).

Praying His Name
To pray in Jesus' name, the Sacrifice That Atones for Our Sins, is to pray in the totality of Christ' unconditional forgiveness. At the heart of the prayer Christ taught His disciples is the petition "forgive us our debts, as we forgive our debtors" (Matthew 6:12, NKJV). The idea of debts here

refers not to money owed, but rather to a "sin debt" owed. The New Living Translation of this verse reads, "And forgive us our sins, as we have forgiven those who sin against us."

If Jesus' name means forgiveness, then praying in Jesus' name means we are praying in the fullness of His forgiveness. If a brother has wronged you, forgive him in your heart. And if God impresses on you to go directly to that brother with a word of forgiveness, don't hesitate.

Place every sin (our own and those of others) under the "blood covering" of Christ. May we deal as decisively with each sin as John Wesley did when he prayed:

Forgive them all, O Lord: Our sins of omission and our sins of commission; the sins of our youth and the sins of our riper years; the sins of our souls and the sins of our bodies; our secret and our more open sins; our sins of ignorance and surprise, and our more deliberate and presumptuous sins; the sins we have done to please ourselves, and the sins we have done to please others; the sins we know and remember, and the sins we have forgotten; the sins we have striven to hide from others, and the sins by which we have made others offend. Forgive them, O Lord, forgive them all for His sake, Who died for our sins and rose for our justification, and now stands at Thy right hand to make intercession for us, Jesus Christ our Lord.[2]

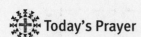 ## Today's Prayer

FATHER, I BOW TODAY WITH A RENEWED SENSE OF GRATITUDE FOR YOUR ALL-ENCOMPASSING PROVISION IN JESUS. IT IS ASSURING TO BE REMINDED THAT MY DEBT OF SIN IS COMPLETELY PAID; MY BROKEN PAST COMPLETELY FORGIVEN; MY LIST OF FAILURES COMPLETELY DESTROYED; MY RECORD OF DISOBEDIENCE COMPLETELY FORGOTTEN. PLEASE ACCEPT MY PRAYER, MY CONFESSION, THAT I SOMETIMES AM OVERCOME BY CONDEMNATION THROWN BY MY ADVERSARY. LORD, TODAY I RISE WITH THE BANNER OF THE BLOOD OF JESUS, TO HURL IT IN THE ADVERSARY'S FACE. IN JESUS' NAME, MY ATONEMENT IS COMPLETE; MY SIN IS COMPLETELY COVERED; I AM COMPLETELY FREE. I AM CIRCLED BY THE SAVIOR'S RIGHTEOUSNESS, CLOTHED IN JESUS' SINLESS EXCELLENCE, REJOICING IN MY FULL ACCEPTANCE. THANK YOU, LORD! IN JESUS' NAME, AMEN.

Day 11 {FORGIVENESS}

MY PERSONAL MEDITATIONS

_____

_____

_____

_____

_____

_____

_____

_____

_____

_____

_____

_____

_____

_____

_____

_____

_____

_____

_____

_____

_____

_____

_____

_____

_____

_____

_____

_____

MORE NAMES FOR JESUS

Check the index beginning on page 162 for these additional names for Jesus that suggest the Sacrifice That Atones for Our Sins: God's Gracious Gift; Holy Sacrifice; Jehovah-Tsidkenu: The Lord Is Our Righteousness; Lamb of God; My Redeemer; Our Passover Lamb; Rich in Unfailing Love; Sacrifice for Sin.

✠ Day 12 {PROTECTION}

A Wall of Fire

*"Then I, myself, will be a protective wall of fire around Jerusalem," says the LORD.
"And I will be the glory inside the city!" Zechariah 2:5*

Do you feel well protected? Most of us don't have the need or means to have a personal bodyguard protecting us. But in reality we actually do, as this next story dramatically illustrates.

More than a hundred years ago a young missionary felt compelled to take the gospel message to a much-neglected—and dangerous—region of China's interior. The area was overrun with ruthless bandits. But the young man didn't let that deter him from his evangelistic mission. He traveled out and back on a dangerous route without incident of any kind.

Soon a rumor began circulating throughout the province that the missionary escaped attack because he was accompanied by an entourage of eleven soldiers. The missionary was stunned by the story. He had definitely made the trip alone. Or had he? Were the soldiers actually angels by his side? And why were there eleven of them?

The answer came more than a month later in a letter written by the missionary's minister back home. After the minister had received word of the unusual circumstances of the young man's journey, he wanted to tell him the rest of the story. "I called a special prayer meeting on your behalf, unaware that it was the same day that you were beginning your journey." Only a few people came to pray, and the minister was disappointed. That is, until he heard the outcome of the missionary's trip. Because, he concluded in his letter to the young missionary, "You'll be pleased to know that, counting myself, there were exactly eleven of us who were praying for you that very day."

Knowing His Name

Whether the missionary was aware of it or not, he had been traveling within the power of one of Jesus' mighty names, a Wall of Fire, a title God gives Himself in Zechariah 2:5.

This promise of protection against enemies takes place during a building project. After seventy years of Babylonian captivity, thousands of Jews had returned to Jerusalem to find that the city was in a shambles. The wall had been broken down and the Temple was completely destroyed.

Under Zerubbabel's leadership, the exiles began rebuilding the Temple. Progress was slow and the workers became discouraged. In addition, without the safety measure of a surrounding wall, the team of builders were vulnerable to the "sniping" of their enemies. It is at this point that the word of the Lord came to the prophet Zechariah, instructing him to tell Jerusalem that "I . . . [God] will be a protective wall of fire around Jerusalem" (2:5).

Zechariah's announcement was a reassuring promise. Zerubbabel and his crew successfully rebuilt the Temple and the opposition against God's people was overthrown.

Living His Name

How does an ancient building project apply to us today? Let's take a closer look at this story to reveal who the recipient of the promise is, and the composition of this new wall.

The promise in Zechariah 2:5 was specifically made to the inhabitants of Jerusalem at that time. However, in Hebrews 12:2, it says that all Christians who make up the church (all who have committed their lives to Christ) have "come to Mount Zion . . . the heavenly Jerusalem." As citizens of the city of God we are assured of the benefits that come with dwelling in this stronghold (see Psalm 48). In this psalm David extols the security and defensibility of Jerusalem because God's presence dwells there (Psalm 48:3). If the Lord promises to be a "wall of fire around Jerusalem" He is also a wall of fire about us today.

What exactly is this fire? It is

*The wall of fire is God's glorious presence encircling His people and **protecting** them.*

the radiance of God's glory—the glory that filled the Tabernacle in Moses' time with bright splendor and flooded the Temple when Solomon dedicated it to the Lord. The Wall of Fire is God's glorious presence encircling His people and protecting them in three unique ways.

First, *a Wall of Fire separates*. In Numbers 16:35, we read the dramatic climax of Moses' confrontation with Korah, an Israelite who was conspiring to overthrow Moses and his brother, Aaron: "Then fire blazed forth from the LORD and burned up the 250 men who were offering incense." God had drawn a line of judgment between His followers and the rebels. And the fire that blazed forth from the Lord was both a protection and a vindication. In the Lord's Prayer, Jesus tells us to pray that God would "rescue us from the evil one" (Matthew 6:13). Jesus is a Wall of Fire who will defend us from the evil one's assaults, confront sin, and destroy it.

Second, *a Wall of Fire insulates*. During the forty-year sojourn of the Israelites in the wilderness, they witnessed God's presence as a covering cloud by day and a pillar of fire by night. God's glory was both visible and

beneficial: it had a cooling effect by day and a warming effect by night. In a similar way, Jesus' name insulates us against the fiery blasts of Satan or the cold chills of spiritual indifference.

Finally, *a Wall of Fire terminates*. Think of it as a police blockade or barricade to contain a violent criminal. God barricades the enemy's advance against us. Exodus 14:19-21 recounts how the fiery cloud of God (His glory fire) walled off Pharaoh's troops who were pursuing the Israelites. The next morning the Israelites crossed safely through the Red Sea.

As a child of God, no matter what you do or where you go, His Wall of Fire surrounds you.

Praying His Name

Praying to Jesus utilizing the name, Wall of Fire, takes you into the fiery enclosure of His presence.

Catherine Siena prayed such a prayer in the fourteenth century:

O eternal Godhead, O sea profound, what more could You give me than Yourself? You are the fire that ever burns without being consumed; You consume in Your heat all the soul's self-love; You are the fire which takes away cold; with Your light You illuminate me so that I may know all Your truth. Clothe me, clothe me with Yourself, eternal truth, so that I may run this mortal life with true obedience, and with the light of Your most holy faith.[1]

Today's Prayer

TODAY, O LORD, I GIVE THANKS FOR YOUR PROMISE OF PROTECTION. AS A WALL OF FIRE, DEAR SAVIOR, PROTECT ME AND DELIVER ME FROM THE EVIL ONE. I COME WITHIN THE SHIELDING PROTECTION OF YOUR INSULATING PROVISION, THANKING YOU THAT THE WALL WHICH SURROUNDS ME IS A COVERING AS WELL. WHEN THE ENEMY SEEKS TO GAIN ADVANTAGE OF ME, MY LOVED ONES, OR ANY OF YOUR OWN WHOM I NAME—IN JESUS' NAME, MY WALL OF FIRE, STOP THE ADVERSARY'S ACTION AND RESTRAIN HIS ADVANCES. MY EYES ARE UPON YOU, MY PROTECTIVE WALL OF FIRE. IN JESUS' NAME. AMEN.

MY PERSONAL MEDITATIONS

_____

_____

_____

_____

_____

_____

_____

MORE NAMES FOR JESUS

Check the index beginning on page 162 for these additional names for Jesus that suggest a Wall of Fire: Devouring Fire; Flame; Jehovah-Shammah: The Lord Is There; Sun and Shield.

✝ Day 13 {VITALITY}

A Life-Giving Spirit

The Scriptures tell us, "The first man, Adam, became a living person." But the last Adam—that is, Christ—is a life-giving Spirit.   1 Corinthians 15:45

Have you noticed how many energy drinks are available in your local grocery store these days? Or the amount of vitamin supplements that offer increased vitality? It seems just when you've seen them all, new ones come out!

Years ago a minister was giving a eulogy at a funeral. Motioning toward the deceased in the casket, the preacher said, "This corpse has been a member of my church for ten years." Sometimes the truth slips out at the most inconvenient times.

The sad truth is that the church appears to be filled with spiritual corpses—people who lack divine vitality. They may attend church, even occasionally read their Bibles and pray, but spiritually, they come up short.

But praise God, those who learn to pray in the energy and vitality of Jesus' name, a Life-Giving Spirit (1 Corinthians 15:45), can be energized by God's essence. God "never slumbers or sleeps" (Psalm 121:4). As Henry Ward Beecher observed, "The most intensely thoughtful and most intensely active being in the universe is God. He is never weary of His work."[1]

Knowing His Name

Stop for a moment, take a deep breath, then slowly exhale. We can't live without being able to breathe. There is a haunting phrase in Isaiah: "Stop trusting in man, who has but a breath in his nostrils" (Isaiah 2:22, NIV). Here God proclaims to His messenger, Isaiah, that a person's strength, pride, and accomplishments are ultimately destined for failure if that person's source of energy is human breath alone. More important is having the life-breath that proceeds from the Spirit of God.

The apostle Paul describes this divine dimension of energy—the breath of the Holy Spirit which proceeds to us through the person of Jesus. "The Scriptures tell us, 'The first man, Adam, became a living person.' But the last Adam—that is, Christ—is a life-giving Spirit. What comes first is the natural body, then the spiritual body comes later. Adam, the first man, was made from the dust of the earth, while Christ, the second man, came from heaven" (1 Corinthians 15:45-47).

All of us are like Adam, depending upon our respiratory systems to survive. God created us that way: "He breathed the breath of life into the man's nostrils, and the man became a living person" (Genesis 2:7). But there is an added dimension of living energy (life-sustaining "breath") available to all whom Jesus has redeemed.

Consider Christ's appearance to His disciples after His resurrection recounted in John 20:22: "Then he breathed on them and said, 'Receive the Holy Spirit'." This is a direct parallel of God's first creation, when the Father created man, giving him the breath of life. Because of Jesus' death and resurrection, a new creation has been made possible. The Lord Jesus Christ—"the Second Adam"—now transmits a life-breath that gives spiritual vitality.

Living His Name

Have you ever been so busy that you actually needed to stop and catch your breath? It certainly is a physical reality, but it can be a spiritual reality too. Reaching that spiritual limit is described in David's words: "As the deer

In Jesus' name we can proclaim death to whatever is robbing us of energy and vitality.

longs for streams of water, so I long for you, O God" (Psalm 42:1). David had the right solution—go to the Lord!

Our Savior is a life-giving Spirit—a revitalizing, breath-of-life-giving "resuscitator" of weary souls. When your spiritual breath rate seems shallow or labored, it's probably a sign that you need "spirit-breath." It's available in Jesus' name, our Life-Giving Spirit.

Praying His Name

To pray in Jesus' name, our Life-Giving Spirit, is to stop periodically and take a deep breath of His fresh, supernatural, "life-giving" air. It is to "catch our breath" in His promise: "But those who trust in the LORD will find new strength. They will soar high on wings like eagles. They will run and not grow weary. They will walk and not faint" (Isaiah 40:31). Spiritual vitality is linked to waiting upon the Lord. St. Francis de Sales in his *Letters to Persons in Religion* suggested centuries ago, "Just walk on uninterruptedly and very quietly; if God makes you run, He will enlarge your heart."[2]

To pray in Jesus' name, our Life-Giving Spirit, is to implement, through prayer, Proverbs 18:21: "The tongue can bring death or life." In Jesus' name we can proclaim death to whatever is robbing us of energy and vitality (whether it be spiritual, physical, or material) and speak life into those same situations or circumstances. For example, we can speak death in Jesus' name to resentment that may be destroying a marriage and speak life into the loving affection that once existed, even though it may seem to have disappeared.

Praying in Jesus' name, our Life-Giving Spirit, is using the power of His name to renew our own spirits each day. It is to pray with the psalmist, "For the glory of your name, O LORD, preserve my life" (Psalm 143:11). Dwight L. Moody made such a petition:

Use me then, my Savior, for whatever purpose, and in whatever way, You may require. Here is my poor heart, an empty vessel; fill it with Your grace. Here is my sinful and troubled soul; quicken it and refresh it with Your love. Take my heart for Your abode; my mouth to spread abroad the glory of Your name; my love and all my powers, for the advancement of Your believing people; and never suffer the steadfastness and confidence of my faith to abate; so that at all times I may be enabled from the heart to say, "Jesus needs me, and I am His."[3]

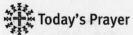 **Today's Prayer**

LORD, I COME TODAY AS YOUR NEW CREATION. I PRAISE YOU FOR THE NEWNESS INTO WHICH YOU'VE USHERED ME—NEW JOY, BECAUSE YOU'VE FORGIVEN ME; NEW HOPE, BECAUSE OF YOUR PROMISES TO ME; AND NEW LOVE, BECAUSE YOU FIRST LOVED ME. BUT LORD, I AM ALSO VERY CONSCIOUS OF MY LIMITS. THOUGH PART OF A NEW CREATION, I AM ALSO A CREATURE OF ADAM'S RACE. MANY TIMES MY SPIRIT IS WILLING BUT MY FLESH IS WEAK. I COME TO RECEIVE THE LIFE-BREATH OF YOUR SPIRIT. YOU BREATHED INTO ADAM LONG AGO, AND THE FIRST CREATION SPRANG TO LIFE. NOW, O LORD—O LIFE-GIVING, QUICKENING SPIRIT—BREATHE FRESHNESS AND NEWNESS OF LIFE INTO MY WEARINESS, AND YOUR SPIRIT STRENGTHEN ME BEYOND MY WEAKNESS. IN JESUS' NAME, AMEN.

MY PERSONAL MEDITATIONS

_____

_____

_____

_____

_____

_____

_____

MORE NAMES FOR JESUS

Check the index beginning on page 162 for these additional names for Jesus that suggest a Life-Giving Spirit: Christ Who Is Your Life; Jehovah-Hosenu: The Lord Our Maker; Living One; Renewer of My Strength; Resurrection and the Life.

14 {BOLDNESS}

The Lion of the Tribe of Judah

But one of the twenty-four elders said to me, "Stop weeping! Look, the Lion of the tribe of Judah, the heir to David's throne, has won the victory. He is worthy to open the scroll and its seven seals."   Revelation 5:5

D o you pray little prayers? big prayers? or both?

"Pray the largest prayers," preached Phillips Brooks. "You cannot think of a prayer so large that God, in answering it, will not wish you had made it larger. Pray not for crutches—pray for wings!"[1]

Hebrews 4:16 gives clear instructions: "So let us come boldly to the throne of our gracious God. There we will receive his mercy, and we will find grace to help us when we need it most." What gives us that confidence? Because we pray in Jesus' name, the Lion of the Tribe of Judah, who "has won the victory" (Revelation 5:5).

Knowing His Name

The context of this verse depicts Christ in His present place of ministry. This is not the picture of the future, it is now! Christ is receiving worship now (see Revelation 5:9–14), and is receiving the prayers of His people now (v. 8). The scroll He takes (5:7) is the "title deed" to this planet. It expresses the fact that "all authority in heaven and on earth" has been given to Him (Matthew 28:18).

It is as the Lion of the Tribe of Judah that Christ has gained this position. He is the fountainhead of our boldness. Because Christ possesses all authority, there is no request concerning anything in heaven (the invisible world) or on earth (physical, personal, material, or even political realm of activity) that is beyond our asking. It is ours in Jesus' name, the Lion of the Tribe of Judah.

Living His Name

To live effectively in Jesus' name, the Lion of the Tribe of Judah, we must recognize that Christ's power as the Lion results from His work as the Lamb (Revelation 5:6). His authority over the works of hell as well as the kingdoms of earth flows from the Cross (see Colossians 2:14–15). Through the Cross and the Resurrection, Christ becomes the fulfillment of Jacob's prophecy to his son Judah, given eighteen hundred years earlier (see Genesis 49:8–12). In Genesis, Judah is likened to a lion that springs forth upon its prey, exactly as Christ came forth from the tomb carrying the keys of death (see Revelation 1:18).

When Jacob spoke this prophecy he declared, "The scepter shall not depart from Judah . . . until Shiloh comes" . . . (Genesis 49:10, NKJV). *Shiloh* is a reference to the coming Messiah, and Jacob's promise to Judah is that he would carry authority until the Messiah came. As the Lion of Judah, Jesus fulfills the prophecy in Genesis 49:9: "He has burst forth from the grave like a lion springing upon its prey" (personal paraphrase)—with His resurrection, Christ "destroy[ed] the works of

Christ's power as the Lion results from His work as the Lamb.

the devil" (1 John 3:8). Christ triumphantly holds the scepter of authority and provides us with boldness in all we do.

So to live today knowing that Jesus is the Lion of the Tribe of Judah is to arm yourself with His boldness. He will spring upon every difficult circumstance we face. And just like a loud roar from a lion frightens away its enemies, a firm "in Jesus' name" spoken boldly over a troubling situation will call Christ's power into action.

Praying His Name

The name *Judah* means "praise" (Genesis 29:35). When Israel went into battle, Judah, the largest of Israel's tribes, was at the forefront bearing the banner before the entire host of Israel (see Numbers 10:14).

How does that apply to us? The best way to apply the power of Christ's name, the Lion of the Tribe of Judah, is through praise. Begin each day's time of prayer with praise. When we proceed into today's battles with praise, the enemy becomes confused and scattered (see 2 Chronicles 20:20-22). Whatever burden we carry is lightened by a spirit of rejoicing and confidence in Christ's victory. As the old camp meeting chorus declares, "The Lion of Judah shall break every chain, and give us the victory again and again!" Praise is essential to victorious prayer.

We must never forget that our adversary "prowls around like a roaring lion, looking for someone to devour" (1 Peter 5:8). But even more important, we must remember he has a worthy opponent in another "lion"—Christ, the Lion of Judah. No wonder the next verse calls for us to stand strong against the devil: "Stand firm against him, and be strong in your faith. Remember that your Christian brothers and sisters all over the world are going through the same kind of suffering you are" (1 Peter 5:9).

Explore God's Word today, searching out new ways to praise and worship Christ, the Lion of the Tribe of Judah. Studying God's Word means you will praise more deeply, and deep praise results in victorious warfare.

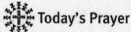 **Today's Prayer**

HALLELUJAH, FATHER! I STAND BEFORE YOUR THRONE WITH PRAISE! LIKE A BANNER
SPREAD BY A TROOP GOING FORWARD IN BATTLE, I LIFT MY PRAISES. JESUS, YOU ARE
MIGHTY! LORD, GOD, YOU ARE VICTORIOUS! SPIRIT OF GOD, LIKE AN ALL-CONSUMING
FLAME, GO BEFORE ME AND FIGHT ALL THAT OPPOSES THE FATHER'S PURPOSE FOR
MY LIFE. YOU ARE JEHOVAH-SABAOTH: THE LORD OF HOSTS. AS THE LEADER OF THE
TROOPS OF HEAVEN, GO BEFORE ME. AS THE LION OF THE TRIBE OF JUDAH, SWEEP
INTO BATTLE AND DEFEAT SATAN WHO SEEKS TO DESTROY ME. WHILE YOU BATTLE ON
MY BEHALF, I BOW TO PRAISE YOUR ALMIGHTY NAME. IN CHRIST I AM MORE THAN A
CONQUEROR. IN JESUS' NAME, AMEN.

MY PERSONAL MEDITATIONS

_____

_____

_____

_____

_____

_____

_____

_____

_____

MORE NAMES FOR JESUS

*Check the index beginning on page 162 for these additional names for Jesus
that suggest the Lion of the Tribe of Judah: Leader among the Nations; Lord
Invincible in Battle; Mighty Right Arm; Triumphant Sword.*

✛ Day 15 {R E S T O R A T I O N}

The Lord Who Heals

He said, "If you will listen carefully to the voice of the LORD your God and do what
is right in his sight, obeying his commands and keeping all his decrees, then
I will not make you suffer any of the diseases I sent on the Egyptians; for I am
the LORD who heals you." Exodus 15:26

We live in a world where "finding the cure" for a growing list of diseases seems to always be in the news. The truth is, the majority of us have a loved one or friend who is need of some type of healing. How that healing occurs is the key.

Years ago, a doctor was surprised to learn that he had been named as a beneficiary in one of his patients' wills. He had treated the woman for nearly four decades, until her death in her nineties. At the reading of the will the doctor was informed that the deceased had left him a large trunk that had been securely padlocked and stored in her attic. Some suspected the chest contained the woman's wealth.

When the trunk was opened, however, the contents weren't coins or currency. Instead, there was forty years' worth of prescriptions, still in their bags, untouched. It was the woman's way of saying, "Thanks, doctor, for your concerns about my health, but I'll just trust the Lord who made my body to heal it."

Knowing His Name

Good health is one of life's priceless blessings. And God certainly has equipped the human body with an unusual capacity to heal itself (provided that it is cared for properly).

Thousands of years before modern doctors began emphasizing "preventative medicine," God told Israel He wanted to spare them the numerous diseases plaguing Egypt (see Exodus 15:22-27). Just three days before, God had brought Israel miraculously through the Red Sea. Now they were traveling in a sweltering desert and found themselves without water. When they finally stumbled upon a pool of water at Marah, they quickly discovered it was unfit to drink. Moses cried out to God in desperation.

The Lord responded by telling Moses to find a branch and toss it into the water. The patriarch obeyed and the waters instantly were purified or "healed." Immediately God told Moses, "If you will listen carefully to the voice of the LORD your God and do what is right in his sight, obeying his commands and keeping all his decrees, then I will not make you suffer any of the diseases I sent on the Egyptians; for I am the LORD who heals you" (Exodus 15:26).

The expression "The Lord who heals" (Exodus 15:26) is derived from the Hebrew word *Jehovah-Rapha*, meaning literally "the Lord Healer." In Jeremiah 8:22 this same Hebrew word is translated *physician*. So Jehovah-Rapha will care for a patient who is ill, but will also give advice to a healthy person on how to stay that way.

The miraculous healing actions of Jesus, the Lord Who Heals, permeate the Gospels. And since Jesus has not changed (see Hebrews 13:8), we can be certain that He cares about *our* sicknesses as well.

Living His Name

Living in Jesus' name, the Lord Who Heals, begins with taking care of our physical body, the earthly temple where God lives (see 1 Corinthians 6:19-20). Any

Christ responds to every level of personal brokenness.

number of things could cause a person's illness—neglect, bitterness, abuse. The first step toward healing is to confess these sins (1 John 1:9). But that's only the beginning. Christ promises health for body, soul, and spirit. He heals broken hearts (Psalm 147:3), He frees mistreated people, (Luke 4:18) and heals us from our waywardness (Jeremiah 3:22). In short, Christ responds at every level of physical, emotional, mental, spiritual, and personal brokenness. As the psalmist said, "He forgives all my sins and heals all my diseases" (Psalm 103:3).

Let's look more closely at the story in Exodus 15:22-27. Symbolically, the bitter waters of Marah could reflect the disappointments of life that can embitter the soul and sour our existence. Consider the Israelite's feeling of disappointment. At a distance they saw what appeared to be a pool of refreshing water. They went from exultation to devastation when they discovered the water was unfit to drink.

It was at this point in the narrative that Jesus' name took effect. God told Moses to find a branch (a symbol of the coming Messiah as prophesized in Jeremiah 23:5, KJV) and toss it into the water. Just as Moses'

branch ultimately healed the bitter waters of Marah, Isaiah's subsequent prophecy (Isaiah 53) predicted the Messiah's suffering on the cross and the healing that would result from His actions.

Praying His Name

To pray today in Jesus' name, the Lord Who Heals, is to pray Jeremiah's prayer with confidence: "O LORD, if you heal me, I will be truly healed" (Jeremiah 17:14). Because Satan, the "prince of death," seeks to rob us of all health, he must be resisted in the power of Jesus' name, the Lord Who Heals.

Armed with God's Word and its promises for victorious, healthy living, we need to apply James' injunction: "Resist the devil, and he will flee from you" (James 4:7).

Interestingly, the Greek word translated "resist" in James 4:7 *(histemi)* is the basis for the word translated, "stand firm" *(anthistemi)* in Ephesians 6:11, where Paul issues a challenge to "stand firm against all strategies of the devil." We need to prayerfully stand firm against all of Satan's strategies which are designed to hinder our health and happiness.

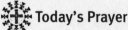 **Today's Prayer**

I CALL UPON YOUR NAME, O LORD, THE LORD WHO HEALS. THANK YOU FOR SENDING
JESUS TO FURTHER REMIND US—TO REMIND ME—HOW GREAT YOUR LOVE IS AND
HOW UNLIMITED IS YOUR HEALING POWER. HEAR MY CRY, FOR I AM SICK, LORD. I AM
SICK IN BODY; I AM WEARY IN SOUL; I AM TIRED IN SPIRIT; I AM IN PAIN. O JESUS,
TOUCH MY BODY WITH HEALTH. LORD JESUS, RESTORE MY SOUL AND REVIVE MY
SPIRIT. HEALING SAVIOR, REMOVE MY PAIN. I CAST ALL THIS BROKENNESS UPON YOU,
WHO SUFFERED IN MY PLACE SO I COULD BE HEALED. WITH PRAISE TO YOU, I RELAX
IN YOUR PROMISES AND POWER, KNOWING ALL WILL BE WELL. YOU ARE MY HEALING
LORD. IN YOUR NAME, AMEN.

MY PERSONAL MEDITATIONS

_____

_____

_____

_____

_____

_____

_____

_____

_____

_____

MORE NAMES FOR JESUS

*Check the index beginning on page 162 for these additional names for
Jesus that suggest the Lord Who Heals: Author of Life; Fountain of Living
Water; God of All Comfort; Hope of My Heart; Jehovah-Ropheka: The
Lord Who Heals You; Medicine in Gilead.*

The Power of God

But to those called by God to salvation, both Jews and Gentiles, Christ is the power of God and the wisdom of God.   *1 Corinthians 1:24*

How much power is in a name? If you're a Gates, a Buffett, or a Trump, your name holds power from not only what you have done but the amount of money you've earned from doing it successfully. But would saying any of those famous names stop a crime from being committed?

Years ago, during a senior class picnic, a student named Pete and his friends had wandered off from the rest of the group, even though they knew the area had been the scene of recent crimes. In the deep woods, the wanderers were startled by members of a gang. Suddenly, there was the flash of a knife in Pete's face.

"I tried to speak the name of Jesus, but I couldn't talk," Pete later told his church youth group. "All I could do was think of the verse, 'Greater is he that is in you, than he that is in the world'" (1 John 4:4, KJV).

Pete continued. "Don't ask me to explain this, but the minute I thought that verse, the guy with the knife started shaking all over, nearly dropping the weapon. He took about three steps backwards and said, 'You're just lucky I'm in a good mood today and am going to let you go.' With that, the gang members practically ran into the bushes."

Knowing His Name

There's something supernatural about the name of Jesus, whether it is thought or spoken. His name is the personification of power. In a word, Jesus' name means "mastery."

Paul introduces us to this idea when he writes that Christ is "the power of God" (1 Corinthians 1:24). This God-given power draws its strength from Christ's sacrifice and victory on the cross, which transcends any human power.

There are numerous words used in the Greek New Testament to describe Christ as the Power of God.

First, *Jesus is our miracle!* Not only does Paul refer to Christ as the Power of God in 1 Corinthians 1:24, but he refers to Christ as "the Son of God when he was raised from the dead *by the power* of the Holy Spirit" in his letter to the Romans (Romans 1:4, italics added). The Greek word translated "power" in these two passages is *dunamis*, from which we get our word *dynamo*. The basic meaning is "extraordinary force" or "supernatural power." Because the word describes that which is "above the ordinary," it is also translated "miracle" in the New Testament. (See Mark 9:39; Acts 2:22; 1 Corinthians 12:10.) In fact, it would not be at all inaccurate to translate 1 Corinthians 1:24 as "Christ, the Miracle of God," for in Him is the consummate and ultimate manifestation of the supernatural. Jesus is not only our power, He is our miracle.

Second, *Jesus is our mastery*. Paul told Roman believers, "For all authority [power] comes from God" (Romans 13:1). John has this to say in his Gospel: "But to all who believed him and accepted him, he gave the right (or the power) to become children of God" (John 1:12). The Greek word translated "power" in these texts is *exousia*. The basic meaning relates to one's privileges or personal rights, but also encompasses a person's influence or sphere of control, including his "mastery" (i.e., his control or authority).

When the disciples said,

Jesus' name is the **personification of power.**

"Who is this man? Even the wind . . . and waves obey him!" (Matthew 8:27), they were amazed at how far Christ's mastery extended—much further than they had realized. Later He transferred that very power to His disciples when He said, "Look, I have given you authority over all the power of the enemy, and you can walk among snakes and scorpions and crush them" (Luke 10:19).

Third, *Jesus is our might*. Two Greek words, *ischus* and *kratos*, describe the sheer strength or might of Christ's power. Paul's second letter to the Thessalonians refers to Christ's coming in "his glorious power [*ischus*]" (2 Thessalonians 1:9). Nothing will be able to withstand Him. "But who will be able to endure it when he comes?" the Old Testament prophet asked (Malachi 3:2). In Revelation, worship is offered to the Lamb, who is worthy to receive "blessing and honor and glory and power [*kratos*] . . ." (Revelation 5:13). *Kratos* describes the aspect of our Lord's might that is so intense that nothing can withstand it. One man-made comparison might be the power of a laser beam. The light of a laser is so concentrated that it can penetrate any object. In Christ, we encounter the concentration (fullness) of all the power of the Godhead (see Colossians 2:9). His might is beyond comprehension.

Finally, *Jesus is our magnificence*. Luke tells us that "awe gripped the people as they saw this majestic display of God's power" when Christ cast out the demon (Luke 9:43). The word here for "power" is *megaleitoes*, which means "magnificence, majesty, or superbness." Here Christ is pictured in His irresistible power, a majestic magnificence that embodies His entire being.

Living His Name

Christ is not only our Miracle, but our Mastery, Might, and Magnificence. Those truths encourage us as we face the uncertainties of this world.

First, wherever we go, whatever we do, *Christ's miraculous power can happen through us*. It may be the miracle of telling our story of faith or the miracle of helping someone who is in need. Each day can become a day of miracles.

Second, we can be assured that *Christ's mastery is more powerful than Satan*. We are in control of our day because Christ is in control, and He dwells within us!

Third, we can face each of today's potential battles knowing that *Christ's might precedes us.* "The battle is not yours, but God's" (2 Chronicles 20:15).

Finally, *we have the joy of living this day saturated with Christ's magnificence.* Anticipate seeing His beauty everywhere—in creation, in circumstances, and even in relationships with others. A hug from a friend, a breath of fresh air, a sunrise or sunset—all will remind us of the magnificence of Jesus.

Praying His Name

Because we live in a culture that bombards us with sinful temptations, believe that the Lord's power can help you overcome every temptation. Are you so tired that you're about to give in? Be honest and tell Him. Allow His magnificence to flood your spirit. If you face a situation that needs a miraculous outcome, cry out to God who made this promise: "Ask me and I will tell you remarkable secrets you do not know about things to come"

(Jeremiah 33:3). Then, with Patrick of Ireland, you can boldly pray: "I bind unto myself today the Power of God to hold and lead, His eye to watch, His might to stay, His ear to hearken to my need."[1]

Especially pray for the miracle of personal spiritual restoration. That is the key to mastery in Christ. Call out to God like Martin Luther did:

Behold, Lord, an empty vessel that needs to be filled. My Lord, fill it. I am weak in the faith; strengthen me. I am cold in love; warm me and make me fervent, that my love may go out to my neighbor. I do not have a strong and firm faith; at times I doubt and am unable to trust You altogether. O Lord, help me. Strengthen my faith and trust in You. In You I have sealed the treasure of all I have. I am poor; You are rich and came to be merciful to the poor. I am a sinner; You are upright. With me there is abundance of sin; in You is the fullness of righteousness. Therefore I will remain with You, of whom I can receive, but to whom I may not give.[2]

Day 16 {MASTERY}

Today's Prayer

YOU WERE THE ONE, LORD JESUS, WHO SAID: "TARRY IN JERUSALEM UNTIL YOU RECEIVE POWER FROM ON HIGH." HERE I AM AT YOUR FEET, LORD. I COME TO YOU, THE FOUNTAIN OF POWER. I HAVE COME TO WAIT . . . AND TO RECEIVE. I NEED YOUR POWER, LORD, BUT I AM SLOWLY LEARNING THAT MY NEED AND ITS SUPPLY ARE DIFFERENT THAN I THOUGHT. I THOUGHT I NEEDED THE ABILITY TO DO THINGS, BUT YOU WANTED TO GIVE ME THE POWER TO BECOME PATIENT, UNDERSTANDING, AND FORGIVING LIKE YOU. I WANTED THE POWER TO CONTROL THINGS, BUT YOU BEGAN TO TEACH ME THAT YOUR POWER, WHICH CREATED ALL THINGS, SUSTAINS ALL THINGS, AND OVERSEES ALL THINGS, IS SUFFICIENT TO MANAGE MY CONCERNS. SO, LORD, I ENTER A NEW DAY OF POWER. YOUR DAY, YOUR POWER, HAVE BECOME MY DAY AND MY JOY. YOUR JOY—WHICH I HAVE GAINED THROUGH YOUR POWER—HAS BECOME MY STRENGTH. HALLELUJAH! IN JESUS' NAME, AMEN.

MY PERSONAL MEDITATIONS

_____

_____

_____

_____

_____

_____

_____

_____

_____

_____

MORE NAMES FOR JESUS

Check the index beginning on page 162 for these additional names for Jesus that suggest the Power of God: Almighty One; Lord God the Almighty; Mighty God; Mighty One.

17 {SECURITY}

A Nail in the Wall

He will bring honor to his family name, for I will drive him firmly in place like a nail in the wall.   Isaiah 22:23

Have you ever been seated next to a first-time flyer on a flight that experiences turbulence? Did you have to reassure your seat mate that the plane wasn't going to crash? What did you say? You certainly could explain that airplanes are constructed to withstand severe turbulence. Once the novice traveler understands the underlying principles of how a plane is designed, it probably will give him peace of mind and a less stressful flight.

The same is true for us understanding Christ's character and the principles concerning the power of His name. If, for example, we understand and put our faith in the principles regarding our security in Christ—the power of His blood over Satan—then we know we are secure under "the shadow of the Almighty" (Psalm 91:1). If, however, we think we're trusting Christ but our faith is weak, we'll be like that first-time flyer.

Knowing His Name

Isaiah 22:23 captures a deeper understanding of the security we have in Jesus' name by uniquely describing our Lord as "a nail in the wall."

In Isaiah's prophecy we find someone who had that security in God. We first meet Eliakim, the palace administrator for King Hezekiah, in 2 Kings 18:18. The dramatic story begins to unfold in 2 Kings 18 and 19, when Jerusalem is threatened by Assyria's king, Sennacherib. Since Hezekiah's allies were feuding, they were not responding to his crisis. Eliakim never wavered from believing that God would deliver them from the Assyrians, while Shebna, the scribe, was soundly cursed for not believing (Isaiah 22:15-19). Eliakim foretold what the Messiah would become to His own. Scripture declares, "I will drive him firmly in place like a nail in the wall" (Isaiah 22:23). In other words, "I will make Him as a secure support for every trophy of victory brought into the house of the living God."

This is a thrilling message! We can be certain that God's enemy will be overthrown; we can be confident that God's victorious trophies will be displayed; and we can draw security from both. We have a "Nail in the Wall."

Living His Name

How often have you heard someone say, "So-and-so *let me down?*" Or maybe you've felt the verbal sting of a *put-down*. Or possibly you are experiencing the *fallout* of a mismanaged company. Each of these phrases describes a negative outcome caused by the inability of one thing to sustain the other.

If someone lets you down, the person is undependable. If someone puts you down, that person is belittling you. "Fallout" describes the negative aftermath of something—originally pertaining to the release of radioactive material into the atmosphere after a nuclear explosion. Let's look at these phrases in light of Isaiah's prophecy about our Nail in the Wall.

Christ has gained us full security through His conquest of sin.

Resting today in Jesus, our Nail in the Wall, helps prevent us from being "let down" no matter what trials we experience. Second, because Christ alone is our security, we don't need to worry about being "put down" by anyone. Finally, there's no negative "fallout" to contaminate our spiritual growth as long as we are confident that Christ truly is our Nail in the Wall.

Praying His Name

To pray in Jesus' name, our Nail in the Wall, is to recognize the full security Christ has gained for us through His matchless conquest of the power of sin, death, and hell. Jesus, through His death, resurrection, and ascension, has "entered the Most Holy Place once for all time, and secured our redemption forever . . . that all who are called can receive the eternal inheritance God has promised them" (Hebrews 9:12, 15). Christ has secured the promise of God's grace, forgiveness, and power toward us. He has entered the temple of God and fastened these provisions with a "nail in the wall." That nail is His own life and blood, two realities that remain as changeless, unshakable, unmovable, infallible, "testimonies of His triumph."

So, to pray today in Jesus' name, our Nail in the Wall, is to enter His courts and lay hold of Him. It is to pray as Vicar John Newman prayed a century ago:

O Lord, support us all the day long, until the shadows lengthen and the evening comes, and the busy world is hushed, and the fever of life is over, and our work is done. Then, Lord, in Your mercy grant us a safe lodging, and a holy rest, and peace at last; through Jesus Christ our Lord.[1]

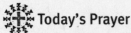 **Today's Prayer**

As I approach Your holy throne today, Father, I thank You that in the holy place of Your dwelling, where I worship You now, there are testimonies surrounding me that represent Your Son, Jesus, and His great victory on my behalf. In the name of Him Whose finished triumph bears never-ending witness, and Whose victory—upon which I hang my hopes for tomorrow—is won, I am secure, knowing this Nail in the Wall will never let me down! I praise You for Your security and Your love that is providing it for me! In Jesus' name, Amen.

MY PERSONAL MEDITATIONS

_____

_____

_____

_____

_____

_____

_____

_____

MORE NAMES FOR JESUS

Check the index beginning on page 162 for these additional names for Jesus that suggest A Nail in the Wall: Fortress; My Support; One Who Guarantees.

A Great Light

The people who walk in darkness will see a great light. For those who live in a land of deep darkness, a light will shine.   Isaiah 9:2

Have you ever been working on a problem and found yourself saying, "Let's try and shed some light on this"? Possibly you are referring to background information you have that would help someone better understand the whole picture. Or you may know future implications of a situation that is driving certain decisions to be made. In either case, "shedding light" means providing guidance. When it comes to your relationship with God, is your heart open to Him shedding His light on you?

In his book *The Electronic Church*, Fulton J. Sheen wrote, "God does not show Himself equally to all creatures. This does not mean that He has favorites, that He decides to help some and to abandon others, but the difference occurs because it is impossible for Him to manifest Himself to certain hearts under the conditions they set up. Sunlight plays no favorites, but its reflection is very different on a lake than on a swamp."[1]

God searches for people who are willing to pull back the curtain of their hearts to let in His beneficial guiding presence—His "Great Light." Quite simply, He is looking for listeners. As François Fenelon cautioned in *The Spiritual Letters*, "How can you expect God to speak in that gentle and inward voice which melts the soul, when you are making so much noise with your rapid reflections? Be silent and God will speak again."[2]

Knowing His Name

Few Old Testament prophets captured the vision of the coming Messiah as completely as Isaiah. Receiving the revelation of the Holy Spirit, Isaiah foretold Christ as: being born of a virgin (7:14); God's chosen servant (42:1); the man of sorrows (53:3); "the Redeemer" (59:20); one who is to be called Wonderful Counselor, Everlasting Father, and Prince of Peace (9:6).

But somehow, amid this list of traits and titles of the Messiah to come, His designation as a Great Light (9:2) seems to be easily passed over as more a prophesied fact than a prophesied feature. Let's think carefully on this aspect of our Savior's personality.

Without pretense of vanity, Jesus told His contemporaries, "But while I am here in the world, I am the light of the world" (John 9:5). These dramatic words were said just as Jesus was about to heal a man blind from birth. You may not have been born with a physical birth defect, but all of us are born with a spiritual "birth defect"—we cannot see clearly the will and way of God for our lives. Our vision becomes clear only when we encounter Jesus Christ. He declares: "I tell you the truth, unless you are born again, you cannot see the Kingdom of God" (John 3:3). In the light of Christ's person, presence, and power we receive the knowledge of God (we perceive His fullness and reality, as well as our need of Him). The psalmist said, "For you are the fountain of life, the light by which we see" (Psalm 36:9).

Living His Name

Scripture uses the image of light to assure us of many blessings vital to spiritual health. None, however, is of greater practical significance to daily Christian living than divine guidance. Frequently the Bible links light with guidance: "Your word is a lamp to guide my feet and a light

God speaks "light" into **the confusion** *and darkness of our daily circumstances.*

for my path" (Psalm 119:105); "The teaching of your word gives light" (Psalm 119:130); "Then God said, 'Let there be light'" (Genesis 1:3).

In the same sense that God "spoke" and light rushed forth to bring about a new world with new growth, God still speaks "light" into the confusion and darkness of our daily circumstances. He responds instantly to show the way, to lead us in His light, to defuse the darkness around us.

Not only is the light "spoken," it is personified. Isaiah's prophecy proclaims that the Messiah is that Light! His presence shines! Where He is, there is light—simply because He is there. To walk in Jesus is to walk in His light.

What does this mean in practical terms? For one thing, consider the reality of this light's penetration. Christ's glow reaches all the way to a "people who sat in darkness." The inference is that a lesser light would not have dispelled the shadows surrounding these people. Scripture declares, "For those who live in a land of deep darkness, a light will shine" (Isaiah 9:2). Has that ever been your experience? All of us have faced those occa-sions when depression, weariness, or criticism has engulfed us like a cloud. But suddenly Jesus—our Great Light—penetrates that cloud with His radiance, and the glow of God's goodness gives us renewed vision.

Not only does the light's power penetrate, it multiplies. Immediately after Isaiah describes the coming Messiah as a Great Light he says, "You will enlarge the nation of Israel, and its people will rejoice. They will rejoice before you as people rejoice at the harvest . . ." (Isaiah 9:3). The message is obvious. When the cloud of oppression is dispelled, growth takes place in the same way that the sun causes a crop to burst into a plentiful harvest.

It's true that a human spirit that is being suffocated by discouragement, disgrace, or disappointment often is incapable of producing fruit. It seems that everything about us withers, fades, and falls like a dead leaf or rotten fruit. One can easily become despondent—overcome by a sense of worthlessness and hopelessness.

But into this desolation the Spirit of God longs to breathe the overcoming testimony of Jesus, our Great Light. This Light brings a brightness, a radiance, and a brilliance of divine ability to transform any circumstance, restoring our purpose and fruitfulness. Our Great Light will multiply, increase joy, and bring a glorious harvest!

Praying His Name

Praying in Jesus' name, a Great Light, means focusing His radiance on the aspects of my day where I need divine guidance. Naturally, this involves prayerful listening. Writing in his *Journals,* Søren Kierkegaard put this in perspective: "The unreflective person thinks and imagines that when he prays, the important thing, the thing he must concentrate upon, is that God should hear what he is praying for. And yet in the true, eternal sense, it is just the reverse; the true relation in prayer is not when God hears what is prayed for, but when the person continues to pray until he is the one who hears what God wills."[3] In other words, only those who linger really listen, for listening takes time.

So, praying in Jesus' name, a Great Light, is to linger long enough in Christ's presence to receive His revelation of God's best for us this moment. His best always begins with a revelation of what needs purifying in our lives. An African child understood this well when he prayed, "O Great Chief, light a candle within my heart that I may see what is there, and sweep the rubbish from Your dwelling place."[4]

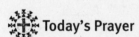 **Today's Prayer**

THIS IS MY SAVIOR, THE LIGHT OF THE WORLD, IN WHOM IS NO SHADOW OF TURNING. NO VARIABILITY, EVER THE SAME, WONDROUS PROVISION IN HIS MATCHLESS NAME, I'M FREE FROM SIN SINCE HE'S TAKEN MY BLAME; NOW WITHIN ME HIS LOVE E'ER IS BURNING.

THIS LIGHT OF ALL LIGHTS SHOWS THE PATH I'M TO TAKE, BE IT THRU BRIGHTEST JOY, DIMMEST SORROW. THE RADIANT PEACE THAT HE GIVES DOTH INSURE, REGARDLESS OF TRIALS, FOREBODING, OBSCURE. IN HIM I'VE A RESTING PLACE EVER SECURE, THAT GIVES GLEAMING HOPE FOR TOMORROW.

Day 18 {GUIDANCE}

THE LIGHT IS THE SAME ON THE MOUNT, IN THE VALE, AND THO' LIFE SEEMS DARK, STILL I KNOW HIS LIGHT HAS NOT FALTERED THRU TESTS OF THE YEARS, IT ONLY SEEMS FLICK'RING WHEN I ALLOW TEARS, TO OVERWHELM ME IN BLACK MOMENTS OF FEAR, THAT BRING GLOOM WHEN TRIAL'S WINDS BLOW.

SO LOOK UP TO HIM, FOR WITH EYES ON THE LIGHT, ONE CAN'T SEE THE SHADOWS SURROUNDING. OVERCAST SKIES WILL THEN SOON BECOME BRIGHT, TEAR-FILLED AND MISTY EYES TAKE ON NEW SIGHT, FOR HIS HAND ON YOUR HEART WILL HIS LOVE-FLAME IGNITE, AND YOU'LL FIND LIFE THAT'S ALWAYS ABOUNDING. (JWH)

MY PERSONAL MEDITATIONS

_____
_____
_____
_____
_____
_____
_____
_____
_____
_____
_____

_____

_____

_____

_____

_____

_____

_____

_____

_____

_____

MORE NAMES FOR JESUS

Check the index beginning on page 162 for these additional names for Jesus that suggest A Great Light: Light of Israel; Light of the City; Light of the World; Light to Everyone; Light to Guide the Nations; My Lamp; True Light; Your Everlasting Light.

The Way, the Truth, and the Life

Jesus told him, "I am the way, the truth, and the life. No one can come to the Father except through me." John 14:6

Did you know at an early age what you wanted to be when you grew up? Did your "plans" actually unfold exactly the way you wanted them to? Can you see how God had His hand on you each and every moment?

The story is told about an old man who was considered the laziest person in the town. When he accepted Christ at a revival meeting, the townspeople wondered if his work habits would be immediately transformed too. Their answer came the following week when the new convert prayed his first public prayer at the midweek prayer meeting: "Use me, Lord, use me—in an advisory capacity!"

God isn't looking for servants to assist Him in an advisory capacity. He has an eternal purpose for everyone who responds obediently to His call. Through Jeremiah God said, "For I know the plans I have for you. . . . They are plans for good and not for disaster, to give you a future and a hope" (Jeremiah 29:11).

Knowing His Name

In *Harvest Time* Charles Spurgeon wrote, "The world is just a materializing of God's thoughts, for the world is a thought in God's eyes. He made it first from a thought that came from His own mighty hand, and everything in this majestic temple He has made has a meaning."[1] Joseph Hall in *The Pleasures of Study* adds, "How endless is that volume which God has written of the world! Wherein every creature is a letter, every day a new page."[2]

You are important to God, a page on which God longs to inscribe in the very signature of His Son a prescription for a life of purpose. That life of purpose begins when we recognize that Christ alone is the Way, the Truth, and the Life (John 14:6). Although each of these names might be defined separately, Christ uses them in reference to Himself in a single statement. This statement can be summed up in a single word—*purpose*.

The Way, the first title on the list, comes from the Greek word *hodos*, defined multiple ways in both the New Testament and Greek literature. It refers to a narrow footpath or a broad road. It also describes highways ("troop trails") soldiers used to march into battle or hold great ceremonial processions. *Hodos* also means the route taken by a ship or the course taken by a river (riverbed).

Christ as our Way suggests someone who is with us in every tight place (narrow path), tempting place (broad road), deep waters, or even wilderness experiences (those dry riverbeds). No matter where we are, the Way is with us! More specifically, when Christ pictured Himself as the Way, He was describing Himself as the One who provides sure footing for our approach to God as well as confidence that we are moving in the right direction. As the Way, Christ also serves as our ever-present guide to God's purposes.

Thomas à Kempis found the Way and sought with all his might to imitate Him. His book *The Imitation of Christ* is perhaps

No matter where we are, Christ, the Way, is with us.

the most widely read Christian devotional. He reflected on Jesus' words:

I am the Way, the Truth, and the Life. Without the Way there is no going; Without the Truth there is no knowing; Without the Life there is no living. I am the Way which thou shouldst pursue; I am the Truth which thou shouldst believe; I am the Life which thou shouldst hope for.

Christ further pictures Himself as *the Truth*. Bible commentator Herbert Lockyer suggests that Jesus qualifies as the Truth because He would not lie. He is the sum total of the truth He taught, He is the guarantee for fulfilled promises, and He reveals truth to every phase of life.[3] Living in Jesus as the Truth means I have help in maintaining my integrity. I have the totality of truth dwelling within me to face life's many demands. I have a living guarantee that His promises to me cannot fail; each situation and phase of life will have validity and meaning. Simply stated, Christ is the way to navigate life's pathways—and that's the truth!

When Christ refers to Himself as *the Life*, He is proclaiming that He is the highest expression

and intent of life. The Greeks used two words for "life": *zoe* and *bios,* from which we derive the words zoology and biology respectively. In the Bible, *bios* relates to man's existence, whereas *zoe* (used in John 14:6) relates to God's purpose and destiny. *Bios* concerns the essential functions of the human being, whereas *zoe* concerns the spiritual and moral qualities of life. Jesus is the ultimate Zoe. Man shares *bios* features with the animal kingdom, but he is designed to know *zoe* in an eternal and abundant dimension. The Bible says, "Whoever has the Son has life [*Zoe*]; whoever does not have God's Son does not have life [*Zoe*]" (1 John 5:12).

Living His Name

Man is special in God's eyes; a creature made "with purpose" to be possessed by the Zoe, Christ Himself. All of earth was designed to prepare man for this purpose. Henry Ward Beecher said in *Royal Truth,* "When God wanted sponges and oysters, He made them, and put one on a rock and the other in the mud. When He made man, He didn't make him to be a sponge or an oyster; He made him with feet and hands, and head and heart, and vital blood, and a place to use them, and He said to him, 'Go, work!' "[4]

To live in Jesus' name, the Way, the Truth, and the Life, is to tap into Christ's zoe-power in every task we undertake. Nothing must be left to chance. Paul told the Corinthians, "So I run with purpose in every step" (1 Corinthians 9:26). Let's find God's plan and purpose for all we experience and declare His name as we move into each task. Take His purpose into family situations, personal relationships, business appointments, and other potentially demanding or even stressful circumstances. We can fill this day, in Jesus' name, with purpose.

Praying His Name

Three centuries ago Bishop Stratford prayed, "O Lord, let me not live to be useless."[5] Christ longs to release usefulness into every day we live. And daily prayer is the place where a true purpose begins.

To pray in Jesus' name, the Way, the Truth, and the Life, is to speak purpose into your day. Boldly offer today's requests knowing you have found the Way, you know the Truth, and you're filled with Life. Your day counts because you have brought God's purpose into it through prayer.

More specifically, you can claim Christ's way for purpose and direction for your family, friends, or even government officials. Pray for Christ's truth to flow into circumstances where Satan, as the father of lies, seeks to sow deeper seeds of deception and untruth. Finally, speak Christ's zoe-power into all areas of potential conflict. Jesus' name means life—abundant life. Saturate your prayers with the fullness of that life!

Praise God for the delight you have in drawing near to God in Jesus' name. How can you be defeated? The Way will guide you, the Truth will guard you, and the Life will undergird you in all you do! Joyfully you can join Desiderius Erasmus in his prayer:

O Lord Jesus Christ, You have said that You are the Way, the Truth, and the Life. Suffer us not to stray from You, who are the Way, not to distrust You, who are the Truth, nor to rest in anything other than You, who are the Life![6]

Day 19 {PURPOSE}

✠ Today's Prayer

Lord Jesus Christ, I come to You today, knowing You are the Way, the Truth and the Life. My prayer is that You would become my Way, my Truth, and my Life. I don't mean that I want You to conform to me, but precisely the opposite. I want to walk my steps in Your Way. I want to think my thoughts in Your Truth. I want my experience to be of Your Life again . . . and again . . . and again. Dear Jesus, I need daily direction as to what to do, instruction as to how to do it, and inspiration to give me ability to get it done. I'm joyfully anticipating when You, the Way (giving direction), and the Truth (giving instruction), and the Life (giving inspiration), make Yourself fully available to be all of that to me, for me, and in me. Thank You, Lord. In Jesus' name, Amen.

MY PERSONAL MEDITATIONS

_____

_____

_____

_____

_____

_____

_____

_____

_____

_____

_____

_____

_____

_____

_____

_____

_____

_____

_____

_____

MORE NAMES FOR JESUS

Check the index beginning on page 162 for these additional names for Jesus that suggest the Way, the Truth, and the Life: Champion Who Initiates and Perfects Our Faith; Chosen One; Eternal Life; Messiah; Mighty Prophet; One and Only Son; Source of Eternal Salvation.

The Word of God

He wore a robe dipped in blood, and his title was the Word of God.

Revelation 19:13

How do you express your creativity? Are you creative with words, with a paintbrush or calligraphy pen, with a lesson plan or sermon delivery? Are you a crafter, a baker, a landscaper, a songwriter, a graphic designer, or a software engineer with endless creative ideas? Where do they come from?

Samuel Taylor Coleridge wrote, "The Hebrew wisdom imperatively asserts an unbeginning creative One who neither became the world, nor is the world eternally, nor made the world out of Himself by emanation or evolution—but willed it, and it was!"[1]

When God willed creation with a word, that Word was actually a person: Jesus Christ. And what a "Word" it was—and is! (See John 1:1 and Colossians 1:15-17.)

To get a glimpse of the incredible creative power of that Word, let's take an imaginary trip across our universe. Our space shuttle will travel fast—at the speed of light, 186 thousand miles per second. We will pass the moon in just 1:3 seconds and leave our solar system in only five hours.

Now the journey gets long. In four years we'll reach earth's nearest star. While zooming through the Milky Way, we arrive at a new star approximately every five years with at least 100 billion stars to go! Traveling in a straight line across the galaxy will take 80 thousand years of continuous travel. (If we were to visit every individual star in the Milky Way, it would take 500 billion years.)

Ready to check out the "neighborhood?" Andromeda, the closest galaxy to the Milky Way, is 2 million years away. Galaxies come in groups, and our group contains approximately seventeen separate galaxies, each with at least 100 billion stars. The largest of the groups in known space is "Hercules," which contains ten thousand separate galaxies. We will reach the first of Hercules's galaxies after traveling 300 million years. When our trip is completed, scientists say, we will have passed some hundred octillion—100,000,000,000,000,000,000,000,000,000—stars. Oh, what a "Word" it was that spoke all of this into being!

Knowing His Name

In Revelation 19:13, John gives a detailed description of the One whose title is the "Word of God." This chapter is loaded with names used to describe Jesus. He is called "LORD" (19:1); "the Lord our God, the Almighty" (19:6, 15); "the Lamb" (19:7, 9); "Faithful" (19:11); "True" (19:11); "the Word of God" (19:13); "King of all kings" (19:16); "Lord of all lords" (19:16); and "God" (19:17).

John introduces Jesus as "the Word" in John 1:1. We read, "In the beginning the Word already existed!" The majestic passage that follows (1:1-18) refers to Jesus as being equal and one with the Father (1:1); as the creator of all things (1:3); as the light that never can be extinguished (1:5); as the One who became human (1:14); and as the One who expressed God's unfailing love and faithfulness (1:17).

Christ's function as Creator, however, is most in evidence when we refer to Him as the Word. He not only made all things but He can make anything even now! John said simply, "God created everything through him, and nothing was created except through him" (John 1:3). The One who dwells within us by the Holy Spirit is the One Who is able to bring worlds into existence with the very breath of His Word. When we pray

Christ often chooses to create through us, His created beings.

"in God's promises"—when we speak what God's Word says, declaring its truth and its resulting hope into a circumstance— we unleash creative potential. This creative power doesn't come from any of us. Rather, it originates from the person of Christ, the Word of God.

Living His Name

Although Christ longs to breathe His creative power into our days, He often chooses to create through us, His created beings. God is the Author of Music, but He gives many of us the gift to compose and perform it. And don't be discouraged if you're not musically inclined. All of us can create a climate of love wherever we go when we carry God's creative Word of love to those in need. To take Jesus' name into our day is to take the "Living Word," Christ Himself, to "comfort the weary" (Isaiah 50:4).

Not only does this Word create, it sustains what it has created. Scripture says that Christ is the One who "sustains everything by the mighty power of his command" (Hebrews 1:3), and that Christ "holds all creation together" (Colossians 1:17). What Christ has called into being He is able to maintain. These

heavens above us and this earth we live on ultimately "will pass away" (2 Peter 3:10-12), and "new heavens and new earth" will be created (2 Peter 3:13). Yet it is a fact that creation still exists right now because Christ has not withdrawn His creative Word (Psalm 148:6).

Think of it! Everything God has created here on earth will eventually become extinct. Everything, that is, but His Word. It shall "never disappear" (Matthew 24:35; Isaiah 40:8). As Peter further reminds us, "That word is the Good News that was preached to you" (1 Peter 1:25). Hallelujah! Because I have become a new person in Christ (2 Corinthians 5:17), my salvation is secure in the Word of God, Christ Himself, and will survive the passing of all creation.

Praying His Name

Not only is Christ, the Word of God, creative, He is the Father's agent riding forth in judgment. His sword (His Word) flowing from His mouth strikes down all evil that prevents the establishment of His eternal kingdom (Revelation 19:11-16). This same Word of God, sent by God, works on our behalf to break the forces of hell that resist His purposes in us. In Christ we have a Savior who creates, sustains, and triumphs.

In Jesus' name we can pray for Christ's creative power to permeate every situation we encounter. When we pray in Jesus' name and present our ideas to Christ, He combines them with His creative genius, resulting in new ideas. Amy Carmichael prayed such a simple prayer:

Holy Spirit, think through me till Your ideas are my ideas.[2]

Believe in the sustaining power of Jesus as you pray today; what Christ has created through your previous prayers of faith He is able to maintain. If you prayed for a situation that improved for a time, but now seems to be deteriorating, speak in Jesus' name for His power to sustain what you claimed earlier in faith.

And don't hesitate to "shout" periodically with a voice of triumph (Psalm 47:1) for Jesus' ultimate victory. Jesus not only creates and sustains, He triumphs! The psalmist challenges us to rejoice, praise, worship, and pray and commands us to shout (Psalm 5:11; 32:11; 132:9).

So find a place where you can lift your voice loudly in triumph over potential troubles. Joyfully exalt Christ, the Word of God, Who creates, sustains, and triumphs through His children.

✠ Today's Prayer

DEAR SAVIOR, I'M GLAD I KNOW YOU AS THE WORD. JUST KNOWING THAT THE ONE WHO MADE ALL WORLDS—WHO WAS THERE BEFORE ANYTHING WAS—IS OVERSEEING MY LIFE, GIVES ME GREAT CONFIDENCE TO STEP INTO THE UNCERTAINTIES OF THIS DAY. LORD JESUS, SPEAK INTO MY LIFE TODAY. SPEAK CREATIVE THOUGHTS. ORCHESTRATE CREATIVE EVENTS. FLOW CREATIVE LIFE. LET YOUR WORDS FLOW THROUGH ME TO HEAL PEOPLE. LET YOUR IDEAS CALL ME TO SERVE OTHERS. AS I AM RENEWED IN YOU, MAY I PRODUCE HOPE WHEREVER I GO, THAT PEOPLE SEE YOU. THANK YOU THAT THE INCARNATE WORD HAS BEEN GIVEN TO ME IN PRECIOUS PROMISES. HELP ME READ THOSE PROMISES AND RECEIVE THEM. BECAUSE YOU ARE THE WORD RESIDING IN ME, MAKE ITS FULLNESS OVERFLOW THROUGH ME. REVEAL YOUR WORD, I PRAY. IN JESUS' NAME, AMEN.

Day 20 {CREATIVITY}

MY PERSONAL MEDITATIONS

_____

_____

_____

_____

_____

_____

_____

_____

_____

_____

_____

_____

_____

_____

_____

_____

_____

_____

_____

_____

_____

_____

_____

_____

_____

_____

_____

_____

MORE NAMES FOR JESUS

Check the index beginning on page 162 for these additional names for Jesus that suggest the Word of God: Creator of All the Earth; Creator of Everything; Exact Likeness of God; Immanuel: God Is with Us; Jehovah-Elohim: The Eternal Creator; Lord Who Created the Heavens.

A Scepter

The message of one who hears the words of God, who has knowledge from the Most High, who sees a vision from the Almighty, who bows down with eyes wide open: I see him, but not here and now. I perceive him, but far in the distant future. A star will rise from Jacob; a scepter will emerge from Israel. It will crush the foreheads of Moab's people, cracking the skulls of the people of Sheth.

Numbers 24:16-17

Are you considered the authority figure in your home? What does that mean to you? What does that mean to your family?

The story is told of an old servant living on a baronial estate in England who regularly used the owner's private path to get to the nearby chapel. The servant was in poor health and the path was shorter and easier. One day an unkind neighbor told the baron what the servant was doing. Sure enough, the baron bumped into the servant one day.

"What right do you have to be on this path?" asked the baron.

"No right at all, sir," the old servant answered. "But I thought you wouldn't mind if an old man used your private path to walk to God's house."

"Give me your walking stick!" the baron said sternly. The man trembled as he handed his stick to the baron. Before the servant could comprehend it, the baron handed him his own walking stick, beautifully adorned with the family crest in solid gold.

"If anyone asks you again what right you have to walk this way," said the baron in a gentle voice, "show them this crest and tell them I gave it to you!"

That is true for us with Jesus, Who has given us the privilege and power to use His name. In Numbers 24:16-17, our Lord is described as "a Scepter" for all those who would choose to live and pray in His name.

Knowing His Name

A scepter is a staff, pole, or rodlike object held by a king or queen as a symbol of royal authority. Scepters come in varied lengths, and, although usually made of wood, they are often covered with precious metal and crowned with jewels. For example, the Royal Sceptre originally made in 1661 (a part of the British Crown Jewels), was redesigned in 1905 to incorporate the Great Star of Africa—a 530-carat diamond. In Psalm 74:2 and Jeremiah 51:19 Israel is described as the Lord's *shaybet,* the Hebrew word for scepter or special possession. In the New King James Version and the New International Version, *shaybet* is translated as "the tribe of [God's] inheritance."

So a scepter may involve more than merely an object—it also can refer to a person in whom authority is vested. This is even true in our time. Today in Britain when an offspring of the monarch is endowed with the same sovereign authority, he or she is "sceptered," or invested with royal authority.

Interestingly, one of the clearest prophecies of the coming Messiah was delivered by an ambivalent character—Balaam. He speaks these words by the Holy Spirit: "A star will rise from Jacob; a scepter will emerge from Israel. It will crush the foreheads of Moab's people, cracking the skulls of the people of Sheth" (Numbers 24:17).

At this time in Israel's

Christ, the Incarnate Scepter, represents God's **total authority** *over all things in this world.*

history, Moab was an obstacle to their wilderness journey. In this prophecy, God proclaimed that this present adversary ultimately would be cast down by a promised Ruler—a Scepter—who would someday rise out of Israel.

Christ is that Scepter of authority. He declared, "I have been given all authority in heaven and on earth" (Matthew 28:18). The apostle Paul writes, "He is the beginning . . . so he is first in everything" (Colossians 1:18). Having been "exalted to the place of highest honor in heaven, at God's right hand" (Acts 2:33), Christ Himself has become the representation—the Incarnate Scepter—of the living God's total authority over all things in this world and in the world to come, including earth, heaven, and even hell itself.

Living His Name

Remember the Old Testament story of Esther? Just as this young Jewess was being crowned the bride of Persia's ruler, King Xerxes (Ahasuerus), the entire Jewish race was scheduled for annihilation. Naturally, Esther wanted to plead for justice and deliverance for her people, but she faced a serious dilemma. Access to the king's court was by invitation only—even for the queen. To enter his throne room uninvited was to risk immediate death. And yet the crisis would not wait for an invitation.

The story's drama builds to that telling moment when Esther ventures into the court on her own initiative. For a few anxious moments the fate of an entire nation hangs in the balance. Suddenly Xerxes acts. He lovingly extends his scepter and invites Esther to approach him and touch it.

When the king extended his scepter, Esther knew she had received his favor, and that her request need only be spoken. The queen touched the symbol of authority and every power was now at her disposal.

Praying His Name

When we come to the Father in Jesus' name, our promised Scepter, we can enter God's holiest of holies. "So let us come boldly to the throne of our gracious God" (Hebrews 4:16). We have a Savior who "understands our weaknesses" (Hebrews 4:15); our most difficult obstacle may be faced in the authority of His name, our Scepter.

When Jesus told His disciples to "ask for anything in my

name" (John 14:13-14), He used a Greek expression that also can mean "make a claim based on my name." The first recorded instance of Christ's disciples "claiming" or "using" His name is found in Acts 3 where Peter and John are at the temple for prayer. As they approach the gate a crippled man pleads for financial aid. Peter boldly assumes an authoritative "prayer stance" (see Acts 3:6), exercising "the power of attorney" Christ gave to His disciples just hours before He went to Gethsemane.

Look carefully at Peter's prayer. He doesn't specifically ask God to do anything in Jesus' name; rather he makes a claim based on Christ's name. He employs the authority of Jesus' name and commands the crippled man to rise and walk. Seconds later, after Peter actually lifts him up (a further act of authority), the man goes "walking, leaping, and praising God" (Acts 3:8).

Exercising our authority in Jesus' name, our Scepter, may go beyond merely asking our Lord to grant a particular request. It may mean we actually command a situation to change in Jesus' name simply because Christ has already given us that authority. He said, "I tell you the truth, you can say to this mountain, 'May you be lifted up and thrown into the sea,' and it will happen. But you must really believe it will happen and have no doubt in your heart" (Mark 11:23).

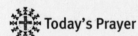

Today's Prayer

Day 21 {AUTHORITY}

MY PERSONAL MEDITATIONS

_____

_____

_____

_____

_____

_____

_____

_____

_____

_____

_____

_____

_____

_____

_____

_____

_____

_____

_____

_____

_____

_____

_____

_____

_____

_____

_____

_____

MORE NAMES FOR JESUS

Check the index beginning on page 162 for these additional names for Jesus that suggest a Scepter: Glorious Crown; King of All Kings; King of the Nations; King over All the Earth; Ruler.

22 {REFUGE}

My Rock

You are my rock and my fortress. For the honor of your name, lead me out of this danger.   Psalm 31:3

What do you think of when you hear the word *refuge*? There are countless wildlife refuges in this country and around the world. People fleeing from war-ravaged areas seek refuge to insure safety and help. Maybe you have a special place that you consider your personal refuge. A private place where you feel safe and peaceful; a place where you can disclose your deepest prayers to God.

In his *Unspoken Sermons,* George MacDonald advised, "That man is perfect in faith who can come to God in the utter dearth of his feelings and desires, without a glow of aspiration, with the weight of low thoughts, failures, neglects, and wandering forgetfulness, and say to Him, 'Thou art my refuge.'"[1]

King David, a man of strong faith, also suffered major setbacks in his life. What David does over and over again is turn to his Lord, My Rock, for refuge (see Psalm 31:3).

In the context of this title David says, "I am dying from grief; my years are shortened by sadness. Sin has drained my strength; I am wasting away from within. . . . I am ignored as if I were dead, as if I were a broken pot" (Psalm 31:10, 12). But David had learned that no matter what the trial, he could pray with assurance, "You are my rock and my fortress. For the honor of your name, lead me out of this danger" (Psalm 31:3).

Knowing His Name

This title for our Lord appears numerous times in Scripture. He is "the rock" (cornerstone) upon which the church is built (Ephesians 2:20). He is our "everlasting rock" (Isaiah 26:4, AMP), translated "Rock eternal" in the New International Version. He is the "towering rock of safety" (Psalm 61:2); "the spiritual rock" (1 Corinthians 10:4); "my rock" and "my fortress" (Psalm 31:3); and "the Rock of my salvation" (2 Samuel 22:47).

As our Rock He shelters, He gives us a foundation, He provides a defense against the enemy, He nourishes and protects us during trials and troubles, and He assures us of a secure footing as we step into each new day. This Rock is an exalted, elevated, out-of-reach location available to the person who takes refuge in Christ's name.

The Hebrew word in Psalm 31:2-3 for "rock" is *sehlah*. *Sela* (from *sehlah*) was the name of an ancient Edomite city. The descendants of Esau called this city "Rock" because it was a natural fortress of refuge. The Greeks later named the city Petra, their word for rock. Petra was virtually impregnable against attack by the military technology and weaponry of the ancient world. The primary access to this stronghold is, as in ancient days, a narrow gorge called the *Sik* (Arabic for "shaft"), which is about a mile in length and approximately ten feet wide. The Sik could easily be defended by a tiny band of people against any invasion. What a powerful picture of our Lord, who is our Rock and Fortress—our hiding place and refuge from every storm.

Living His Name

In these uncertain times, we can face each storm securely in Jesus' name, our Rock. Be encouraged by the fact that we not only dwell in the Rock but the Rock dwells in us. The Fortress is within us!

Psalm 31:2-3 describes the Lord not only as our "rock" and "fortress" but as our "rock of protection." The Hebrew words used here are *metsoodaw* (fortress)

We not only dwell in the Rock, the Rock dwells in us.

and *maoz* (refuge, protection). When combined they describe "a place of escape or defense; a city that, should the enemy seek to overthrow it, he himself will be overthrown." In this sense the words convey a snare or a trap.

Think of it! The traps Satan places before us today will be turned by Christ into traps that will snare Satan himself.

Interestingly, in the same way that *sehlah* (rock) brings the city of Petra (Sela) to mind, so *metsoodaw* (fortress) brings the famous natural fortress Masada (derived from *metsoodaw*) into focus. Masada was a towering natural fortress used by Herod the Great as a military outpost just before the time of Christ. The fortress was built on a butte or mesa, which rises more than fourteen hundred feet above the level of the nearby Dead Sea. It was here in AD 70 to 73 that Jewish zealots sustained a revolt against the Roman Empire. They resisted Rome three years longer than any other of their guerrilla forces simply because of the strength of their position in the Masada.

In a similar way, we too may sometimes feel weak and weaponless as we face our adversary. But we must never forget our position is in Christ, our *Sehlah Metsoodaw!*

Praying His Name

To pray today in Jesus' name, our Rock, is to pray recognizing that Christ is our refuge for every situation we might face. Storm clouds often appear well before a storm, so it's wise to take time in prayer scanning for telltale signs of difficulty. If we sense a storm is developing, we can bring the power of Christ, our Rock, into that situation. If the storm looks severe, the farther into the Fortress we'll need to go to spend extra time resting in our Rock.

When Jesus taught us to pray "rescue us from the evil one" (Matthew 6:13), He was instructing us to assume a warfare stance in prayer. This stance doesn't necessarily mean rushing headlong into battle as much as a prompt retreat into our strong fortress, Christ Himself (Proverbs 18:10).

As we pray, we are fighting our battles from God's throne room where we "sit together" with Christ "in heavenly realms" (Ephesians 2:6). And because God inhabits the praises of Israel, His people (Psalm 22:3), the best way to insure that God's presence "is enthroned" in our prayers is to fill them with praise.

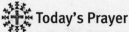 **Today's Prayer**

LORD, I PRAISE YOU BECAUSE "MY HOPE IS BUILT ON NOTHING LESS, THAN JESUS' BLOOD AND RIGHTEOUSNESS; I DARE NOT TRUST THE SWEETEST FRAME, BUT WHOLLY LEAN ON JESUS' NAME. WHEN DARKNESS VEILS HIS LOVELY FACE; I REST ON HIS UNCHANGING GRACE; IN EVERY HIGH AND STORMY GALE, MY ANCHOR HOLDS WITHIN THE VEIL. ON CHRIST THE SOLID ROCK, I STAND; ALL OTHER GROUND IS SINKING SAND, ALL OTHER GROUND IS SINKING SAND."

MY PERSONAL MEDITATIONS

_____

_____

_____

_____

_____

_____

_____

_____

_____

_____

_____

_____

MORE NAMES FOR JESUS

Check the index beginning on page 162 for these additional names for Jesus that suggest My Rock: Refuge for His People; Safe Refuge; Spiritual Rock; Towering Rock of Safety.

The Commander
of the Lord's Army

"I am the commander of the Lord's army." At this, Joshua fell with his face to the ground in reverence. "I am at your command," Joshua said. "What do you want your servant to do?"   Joshua 5:14

For years, the most memorable phrase from the opening credits of ABC's *Wide World of Sports* was "the thrill of victory . . . and the agony of defeat!" For an athlete, victory is definitely thrilling. But even more thrilling for God's people is the fact that God's victories are never ending.

Victories for God's people come in all shapes and sizes. Sometimes it even seems that God sets up certain situations to show His sovereignty. From His vantage point the view is always victorious. As Jonathan Edwards explained in *A History of the Work of Redemption:*

God, doubtless, is pursuing some design and carrying on some scheme in the various changes and revolutions which from age to age come to pass in the world. It is most reasonable to suppose that all revolutions, from the beginning of the world to the end of it, are but the various parts of the same scheme, all conspiring to bring to pass that great event which the Great Creator and Governor of the world has ultimately in view.[1]

Knowing His Name

God's ultimate view of victory is summed up in a person: the Lord Jesus Christ. As we live and pray in Jesus' name, we come to the title: the Commander of the Lord's Army (Joshua 5:14).

Let's take a look at the context. The people of Israel have crossed the Jordan River and are approaching the city of Jericho. When Joshua was scouting the enemy's well-fortified city, the Lord appeared to him (Joshua 5:13-15), identifying Himself as Commander of the Lord's Army (or "Captain of the LORD's host," KJV). Just after this encounter, God issues Joshua a list of unusual steps for his people to take in order to secure victory at Jericho (see Joshua 6:1-5).

As the Commander of the Lord's Army, Christ came into Israel's conflict to work the will of God. The same is true for us. The victories the Lord wants to give us require that we are both committed and submitted to His plans and purposes, rather than persuaded by our own opinions or interests.

Jesus Himself is a beautiful example of this submissive spirit: "God, for whom and through whom everything was made, chose to bring many children into glory. And it was only right that he should make Jesus, through his suffering, a perfect leader [the Greek *archegos*, also meaning 'captain'], fit to bring them into their salvation" (Hebrews 2:10). The pathway to victory often goes through a valley of sorrow or suffering. But we have this unshakable hope: Jesus knows precisely what to do!

Living His Name

As the Commander of the Lord's Army, Christ directs those armies of heaven, innumerable angels by earth's accounting, to serve our interests (Hebrews 1:14).

In the New Testament an equivalent title for Commander of the Lord's Army is Jehovah-Sabaoth or "Lord of Heaven's Armies" (Romans 9:29; James 5:4). Charles Spurgeon

To be victorious, we need to be both committed and submitted to **Christ's plans** *and purposes.*

explained this title: "The Lord (Jehovah-Sabaoth) rules the angels, the stars, the elements, and all the hosts of heaven and the heaven of heavens is under His sway. The armies of men, though they know it not, are made to subserve His will. As the General of the forces of the land, the Lord High Admiral of the seas, Christ is on our side—our supreme ally; woe unto those who fight against Him, for they shall flee like smoke before the wind when He gives the word to scatter them."[2]

Isaiah 37:36 tells of a remarkable example of this angelic power. A lone angel at the direction of the Supreme Commander destroys a vast army in a single night. Think of it! These heavenly messengers are now at our disposal. Little wonder Luther could write:

Did we in our own strength confide, Our striving would be losing. Were not the right Man on our side, The man of God's own choosing. Don't ask who that may be? Christ Jesus, it is He; Lord Sabaoth His name, From age to age the same, And He must win the battle.[3]

Praying His Name

What Joshua learned before the battle of Jericho (Joshua 5:13–6:27) is valuable to us for living and praying effectively in the name of the Commander of the Lord's Army.

First, *never enter a battle without consulting the Commander*. The victory God wants us to experience in Jesus' name depends on receiving the Commander's battle plan. Like Joshua, we need a face-to-face encounter with Christ in personal prayer. We shouldn't expect God to speak to us if we're not available to listen.

Second, *reverently and humbly worship the Lord before seeking His guidance*. Joshua fell on his face humbly before God as an act of worship and reverence before he asked, "What do you want your servant to do?" (Joshua 5:14).

Third, *strive for personal purity after encountering Christ*. If we listen carefully during our time with the Lord, we'll surely hear Him say as He did to Joshua, "Take off your sandals, for the place where you are standing is holy" (Joshua 5:15). Purity is essential to productive praying. Scripture reminds us that it is the prayer of "a righteous person [that] has great power and produces wonderful results" (James 5:16).

Fourth, *only those who listen and obey will experience the totality of Christ's promised victory.* Joshua not only listened to what his Commander said, he obeyed Him down to the last detail. Obedience is the key to victory. Nothing delights or honors God more than an obedient spirit.

Go courageously into battle today to conquer in the name of Jesus, the Commander of the Lord's Army. Pray along with Francis of Assisi:

You are holy, Lord, the only God, and Your deeds are wonderful. You are strong, You are great. You are the most high, You are almighty. You, holy Father, are King of heaven and earth. You are Three and One, Lord God, all good. You are good, all good, supreme good, Lord God, living and true. You are love, You are wisdom. You are humility, You are endurance. You are rest, You are peace. You are joy and gladness, You are justice and moderation. You are riches, and You suffice for us. You are beauty, You are gentleness. You are our protector, You are our guardian and defender. You are courage, You are our heaven and our hope. You are our faith, our great consolation. You are our eternal life, great and wonderful Lord, God Almighty, Merciful Savior.[4]

 ## Today's Prayer

LORD, I PRAISE YOU BECAUSE ON THE CROSS YOU BATTLED EVIL FOR ME AND SECURED THE VICTORY! NOW YOU, AS THE COMMANDER OF THE LORD'S ARMY, ARE BESIDE ME AS I FACE MY BATTLES EACH AND EVERY DAY. HELP ME TO REMEMBER THAT THE BATTLE IS NOT MINE, IT IS THE LORD'S. IN YOUR VICTORIOUS NAME, I PRAY. AMEN.

Day 23 {VICTORY}

MY PERSONAL MEDITATIONS

_____

_____

_____

_____

_____

_____

_____

_____

_____

_____

_____

_____

_____

_____

_____

_____

_____

_____

_____

_____

_____

_____

_____

_____

_____

_____

_____

_____

_____

MORE NAMES FOR JESUS

Check the index beginning on page 162 for these additional names for Jesus that suggest The Commander of the Lord's Army: Coming One; Jehovah-Sabaoth: The Lord of Heaven's Armies; Mighty Warrior; Perfect Leader; Warrior.

24 {SUPERVISION}
The Head of the Body

Christ is also the head of the church, which is his body. He is the beginning, supreme over all who rise from the dead. So he is first in everything.

Colossians 1:18

Do you work for or consider yourself to be a "hands on" or "hands off" boss? Most people tend to be more comfortable with a boss who gives them an assignment to do, then lets them run with it. Working together, using individual strengths, produces results. That's illustrated in the following story.

At a trial, an architect was being cross-examined about a building he had designed. One of the prosecutors asked, "Are you a builder?"

"No, sir, I'm an architect."

"But aren't a builder and an architect interchangeable?" the prosecutor prodded.

"Sir, in my opinion they are totally different."

"How so?"

"An architect conceives the design, prepares the plan, draws up the specifications—essentially an architect supplies the mind behind the project. The builder is the tradesman: the bricklayer or the carpenter. The builder is the machine; the architect, the power that puts it together and sets it going."

"And now, Mr. Architect, perhaps you can inform the court who was the architect of the Tower of Babel?"

The witness didn't hesitate. "There was no architect, sir, only builders. That's why there was so much confusion."

God knew the church needed a head. For this reason Christ was given as the Head of the body. He is our supervisor. And being the Head, He also is our mind or "the brains of the operation."

Christ supervised Creation itself. Scripture states, "for through him God created everything in the heavenly realms and on earth" (Colossians 1:16). In his essay "On the Existence of God," François Fenelon wrote, "Let us study the visible creation as we will; take the anatomy of the smallest animal; look at the smallest grain of corn that is planted in the earth, and the manner in which its germ produces and multiplies; observe attentively the rosebud, how carefully it opens to the sun, and closes at its setting; and we shall see more skill and design than in all the works of man."[1]

Knowing His Name

If you ever travel to London and pass through Paddington Station, one of the primary train terminals, look for the statue of Paddington Bear. Like Winnie the Pooh, Paddington Bear is a favorite children's character, a bear said to have arrived from darkest Peru, with no identification except a tag reading, "Please look after this bear."

There is something touching about these words. Don't we all want someone to look after us? It isn't just a children's need; even adults know that a person never outgrows the need for supervision. That watchful and authoritative supervision is a distinct function of Christ's ministry. As Scripture states, "Christ is also the head of the church, which is his body" (Colossians 1:18).

The first thing that usually comes to mind with this title of our Lord is His right to administrate and direct the affairs of His whole church. Whether we are dealing with the church globally or in a local congregation, Christ is the Architect, Builder,

We can see things as Jesus sees them if we look through His eyes.

and Lord. But the words, "head of the church, which is his body" (Colossians 1:18) also clearly include Christ's personal headship over each member of His body. In the same way that the Bible describes the husband as "the head of his wife" (Ephesians 5:23), pointing out that he is lovingly responsible for her best interests, so Jesus, our Head, is fully committed to each of us who constitute His bride—the church.

Headship doesn't give a person the right to be indifferently bossy or cruelly insensitive to those under his supervision. That misconception can carry over to how we perceive Jesus, too—causing us to actually fear to acknowledge Him as our Head. Such fear might prevent bringing certain details to Him in prayer because we have been exploited by human supervisors and we feel Christ may do the same thing.

If you are struggling with that fear in your relationship with God, think of your physical body's relationship to your physical "head."

Your head—the core of your powers of reason and reflex—is a prime example of the care and concern for the body which any sane, sober head employs. The fact that your head has the power of control over your body does not make your head indifferent or insensitive to your body's needs, feelings, or fulfillment. To the contrary, your head: (1) thinks of ways to make your body better (brings improvement); (2) sees things that might injure or harm your body and avoids them (provides protection); and (3) designs ways and programs that will serve your body's needs (gives assistance). Consider those activities of your head—improvements, protection, and assistance—and then ask yourself, "Is Jesus less thoughtful about His body than I am of mine?"

Living His Name

Jesus, the Head of the Body, is always with us no matter where we go. Though this ever-present "supervisor" most often stands beside us in silence, He is nonetheless present, available on a moment's notice to those who would simply acknowledge His nearness.

As Søren Kierkegaard wrote in his *Journals:* "The remarkable thing about the way in which people talk about God, or about their relation to God, is that it seems to escape them completely that God hears what they are saying."[2]

To live recognizing that Jesus is the Head of the Body is to live with a continuing realization that we are an organic part of that body. Our health depends on supervision from our Head. This involves far more than a mere casual communion with Christ. Consider the components of the word *supervision*. *Vision* refers to the capacity and ability to perceive or see; *super* means "from above." Because Jesus is with us today, we have the capacity to "see from above." We can see things as Jesus sees them if we look through His eyes. Thus, to rely on Jesus, the Head of the Body, is to rely on His supervision in all we do.

Praying His Name

Teresa of Avila, the sixteenth-century "praying nun," founded a spiritual order of nuns called "the barefoot Carmelites." She sought women who possessed a passionate hunger for more of God and a willingness to work with all their might.

One of Teresa's shortest recorded prayers reveals both her blunt nature and her own frailties: "God preserve us from stupid nuns!" Equally brief was her practical prayer, "From silly devotions and from sour-faced saints, good Lord deliver us."[3]

Yet it was this giant of the faith who, at a dark time in an indulgent church, realized Christ had no other means but His church to change the world. And so she cautioned her Order:

Christ has no body now on earth but yours; yours are the only hands with which He can do His work, yours are the only feet with which He can go about the world, yours are the only eyes through which His compassion can shine forth upon a troubled world.

Christ has no body now on earth but yours.[4]

To pray today in Jesus' name as our Head is to acknowledge Him as the supervisor of everything we undertake. Christ alone is the Architect and Builder of our days. In Him there will be no towering Babel of confusion, for "God is not a God of disorder but of peace" (1 Corinthians 14:33).

Today's Prayer

SAVIOR, I'M SO GLAD THAT I'M JOINED TO YOU. WHAT CONFIDENCE I AM PRIVILEGED TO ENJOY, LORD JESUS, SINCE YOU HAVE MADE ME ONE WITH YOURSELF. AND, ACCORDING TO THE FATHER'S WORD, I AM COMPLETE IN YOU! I ENTER THIS DAY, WITH ITS CHALLENGES, ITS PROBLEMS, ITS UNKNOWNS, KNOWING I AM LINKED TO YOU. YOU ARE MY HEAD—ABLE TO DIRECT ME, READY TO PROTECT ME, CERTAIN TO HELP ME, AND FAITHFUL TO NURTURE ME. WITH PRAISE TO YOU, THE DOORWAY TO TODAY OPENS BEFORE ME, AND I HAVE NO HESITATION ABOUT WALKING FORWARD. EACH STEP IS DIRECTED BY YOU—MY LIVING HEAD—MY LORD AND SAVIOR, JESUS CHRIST. IN YOUR NAME, AMEN.

MY PERSONAL MEDITATIONS

_____

_____

_____

_____

_____

_____

_____

_____

_____

_____

MORE NAMES FOR JESUS

Check the index beginning on page 162 for these additional names for Jesus that suggest the Head of the Body: Head of Every Man; Head over All Things; Master of the House; My Helper.

The Expression of the Very Character of God

The Son radiates God's own glory and expresses the very character of God, and he sustains everything by the mighty power of his command. When he had cleansed us from our sins, he sat down in the place of honor at the right hand of the majestic God in heaven.   Hebrews 1:3

Have you ever heard someone describe a child as "the spitting image of his father"? Essentially they are saying that the child is the perfect likeness of that parent. Even more so than children, that is true about our Lord.

Anyone who wants to see God can look at Jesus. Paul reminded the Colossian believers, "And now, just as you accepted Christ Jesus as your Lord, you must continue to follow him. . . . For in Christ lives all the fullness of God in a human body" (Colossians 2:6, 9). John, in referring to Christ as the Word, clearly equated Christ with God. He wrote, "In the beginning the Word already existed. The Word was with God, and *the Word was God*" (John 1:1, italics added). Just as God is real, so Christ is real—the literal "image of the person of God."

It's sad that some people reject God's existence—and His Son—simply because believing is the first step toward submitting to His rule. In *Visions of Heaven and Hell,* John Bunyan said, "When wicked persons have gone on in a course of sin and find they have reason to fear the just judgment of God for their sins, they begin at first to wish that there were no God to punish them; then by degrees they persuade themselves that there is none; and they set themselves to study for arguments to back their opinion."[1]

Knowing His Name

The author of Hebrews not only introduces us to Christ, the Radiance of God's Glory (see Day 7), but also to Christ, the Expression of the Very Character of God (Hebrews 1:3).

In the New King James Bible the title is introduced by the phrase *"who being."* This emphasizes the fact that it is Christ's nature simply "to be." He said, "Before Abraham was, I AM!" (John 8:58). Christ not only exists, He cannot be anything other than what He is. And He is all that He is all of the time. It is His nature to always be the things He is being right now; this is not temporary.

Consider the Greek word *charakter,* meaning "image." The English word *character* is derived from it. This word includes several unique meanings that directly apply to our understanding of Christ, the Expression of the Very Character of God.

First, *character or image describes a mark or stamp that is engraved, etched, branded, cut, or imprinted.* This would include the brand used on a horse or a cow, or an impression on a coin. It is also the word used to describe a stamp or seal embossed on a document.

Second, *this word is used to describe the mark of the Antichrist* imprinted on hands and foreheads of his adherents (Revelation 13:16).

Third, *this is the word used in representative art.* This is art in which a figure or design in a painting or sculpture is meant to represent something that is real in the physical realm. This "image" represents to the viewer what actually and readily exists in another realm.

When we apply these definitions to Christ, the comparisons are exciting. Jesus came as the physical, actual, and original image of God (the very image God originally intended to be upon man) to restamp us with God's image. He, alone, is able to be that "perfect [holy] representative" of the God of the ultimate realm—"ultimate" meaning

Being "branded" by the stamp of
Christ's likeness,
we become God's possession once again.

eternal (as opposed to temporal) and holy (as opposed to fallen and sinful).

What does that mean for us? Being "branded" by the stamp of Christ's likeness, we become God's possession once again. As the sheep of His pasture, we carry His brand! The mark of the antichrist spirit of the world won't work on us because we've been stamped with Christ's character forever. Like a stamp on an envelope, we have evidence that a certain destiny has been chosen on our behalf and that the price of our delivery has been paid.

Finally, we must not overlook the significance of the expression of Christ's person. From the Greek word *hupostasis* comes a phrase that means Christ is "the exact stamp of the reality of God the Father and the perfect essence of Who the Father literally is."

Hupostasis principally means "something that stands under" and therefore gives perfect impression of that which is above it. Christ is the sum of all that God is like and about. As Jesus stands on earth before mankind He is the perfect impression of the nature and character of God the Father. Christ leaves a full-

size stamp; He is the Expression of the Very Character of God.

Living His Name

In the jungles of Africa, through a personal revelation of God's glory, Samuel Morris eventually became a follower of Christ at the end of the nineteenth century. Talking with a missionary, Sammy learned that God carried out His work on earth through His "divine agent," the Holy Spirit. When Sammy asked the missionary how he knew so much about this "Holy Spirit" the missionary explained he had learned about these things at Taylor University in the United States of America.

Sammy promptly asked for directions to this very special place called Taylor University. Amazed, the missionary quickly explained it would be necessary for Sammy to write to Taylor University and request an application for enrollment. When Sammy mailed it back, it would be evaluated to determine if the young man could become a student. With the help of the missionary, the young convert wrote to the university. When the application arrived, the missionary told Sammy there was one last step:

Sammy needed to have his photograph taken to send with the application. When Sammy saw the first-ever photo of himself, the young Liberian insisted that the picture couldn't possibly be of him. Surely someone had made a mistake. When the missionary finally convinced Sammy that the picture was really him, the young African started to cry. He was convinced that the university would never accept him. With tears streaming down his face, Sammy softly explained, "My picture is too ugly. Oh, that I could send them a picture of Jesus."

That is exactly what we can do. When we live in Jesus' name, the Expression of the Very Character of God, we will conduct the business of our days in such a way that we reflect the beauty of Christ Himself. We will give our world a picture of Jesus wherever we go. And the more of Jesus that permeates our being, the clearer the picture of Him will be.

Praying His Name

God desires to stamp our petitions with the imprint of His Son's reality. He longs to impress the mark of Christ's nature and character into everything we do. As we pray today in Jesus' name, the Expression of the Very Character of God, pay attention to the beginning of the Lord's Prayer: "Your kingdom come. Your will be done" (Matthew 6:10, NKJV). To pray "Your Kingdom come" in all we do today is to declare God's imprint in every part of our day. It is to proclaim Christ's lordship over family, work, relationships, and even future plans and goals. It is to ask the Lord to mark every moment with the imprint of Jesus' name—our Expression of the Very Character of God!

 Today's Prayer

Lord, I pray today with the hymn writer who honored You with his song: "O to be like Thee, Blessed Redeemer, This is my constant longing and prayer; Gladly I'll forfeit all the earth's treasure, Jesus Thy perfect likeness to wear. O to be like Thee, O to be like Thee, Blessed Redeemer, pure as Thou art. Come in Thy sweetness, Come in Thy fullness. Stamp Thine own image deep on my heart."

Day 25 {REALITY}

MY PERSONAL MEDITATIONS

_____

_____

_____

_____

_____

_____

_____

_____

_____

_____

_____

_____

_____

_____

_____

_____

_____

_____

_____

_____

_____

_____

_____

_____

_____

_____

_____

MORE NAMES FOR JESUS

Check the index beginning on page 162 for these additional names for Jesus that suggest the Expression of the Very Character of God: Branch of the Lord; Faithful and True Witness; Great Mystery of Our Faith; My Servant; Son of the Most High; True God; Visible Image of the Invisible God; Witness to the People.

✝ Day 26 {ENLIGHTENMENT}
The Wisdom of God

But to those called by God to salvation, both Jews and Gentiles, Christ is the power of God and the wisdom of God. 1 Corinthians 1:24

Do you consider yourself an enlightened person? According to the dictionary, if you are "enlightened," you are "freed from ignorance or misinformation." If a judge issues an "enlightened" ruling, it is "based on full comprehension of the problems involved." In other words, you act wisely because you know the truth.

Paul told the Ephesians, "I pray for you constantly, asking God, the glorious Father of our Lord Jesus Christ, to give you spiritual wisdom and insight so that you might grow in your knowledge of God"(Ephesians 1:16-17). His intercession further asks that "your hearts will be flooded with light so that you can understand the confident hope he has given to those he called—his holy people who are his rich and glorious inheritance. I also pray that you will understand the incredible greatness of God's power for us who believe him" (Ephesians 1:18-19).

God is always longing to enlighten His children concerning Himself, at least to the degree that His children are capable of being enlightened. Phillips Brooks observed: "Remember, God is teaching you always just as much truth as you can learn. If you are in sorrow at your ignorance, then . . . you must not despair. Be capable of more knowledge and it shall be given to you."[1]

God truly knows more than we will ever know, and His ways are clearly above our ways (Isaiah 55:8). He is infinite in wisdom and knowledge and has chosen to reveal all His wisdom through the person of His Son, Jesus Christ, whom Paul pictures as the Wisdom of God.

Knowing His Name

Paul not only introduces Jesus to us as the "power of God" (1 Corinthians 1:24) but in the next breath he calls Him "the Wisdom of God." Six verses later the apostle tells us Christ became for us wisdom from God. The Greek word used here for wisdom is *sophia*. Christ is not just wisdom; He is the Wisdom of God. Man's attempt to obtain wisdom from his own efforts is always lacking. True wisdom comes only from the originator of wisdom, the Creator Himself. That's why the author of Proverbs links all wisdom to God with such statements as "Fear of the LORD is the foundation of wisdom" (Proverbs 9:10). *The Living Bible* paraphrases this: "The reverence and fear of God are basic to all wisdom." Only the Creator can create wisdom, and in Christ He not only sent wisdom to us, but He caused Christ to become wisdom *in* us.

Wisdom and knowledge, of course, are not the same. Knowledge is the comprehension or informational side of a matter, whereas wisdom is the practical and operational side of it. Wisdom is knowing how to do what needs to be done. It is the insight into making something work properly, to making it functional.

We live in an information-based society. People know what they want to do, and even what they ought to do, but they don't know how to do it in such a way to "make life work." But in Jesus' name as the Wisdom of God we discover Christ is our resource of wisdom Who will make life work. He'll show us how to make the details of the day (and the primary issues of our lives) function smoothly and properly.

To impart this wisdom Christ has given us His Holy Spirit, the agent of all divine revelation (2 Peter 1:20-21). "He will teach you everything," Jesus told us (John 14:26). Paul wrote the Colossians, "In him lie hidden all the treasures of wisdom and knowledge" (Colossians 2:3), treasures revealed by the operations of the Spirit of wisdom, God's Holy Spirit.

We cannot live the Word if we don't read the Word.

Living His Name

Wisdom is "the right use of knowledge." Living today in Jesus' name, the Wisdom of God, is trusting Christ's presence to help us apply what we've already learned in Him. First, we must know the promises of God as revealed in His Word. Spending time in God's Word every day is essential to living effectively in Jesus' name.

There may be occasions when God will speak His miraculous wisdom into situations by His Spirit. Paul referred to this gift of the Spirit as "the ability to give wise advice" (1 Corinthians 12:7-8).

Equally exciting is the way the psalmist pictures God's creative acts as expressions of His wisdom. God knows how to bring things which presently do not exist into being. We read, "O LORD, what a variety of things you have made! *In wisdom* you have made them all" (Psalm 104:24, italics added). Note, also, "To Him who by wisdom made the heavens . . . who laid out the earth above the waters . . ." (Psalm 136:5-6, NKJV). In Christ, who is the Wisdom of God, we will discover the creative power of God, which literally functions moment by moment through us as we live in Jesus' name!

Praying His Name

You've probably discovered that many names and titles of Christ seem interchangeable. Christ, for example, is our Wonderful Counselor, providing daily insight; our Great Light, giving daily guidance; and the Wisdom of God, ever enlightening us in His Word. Jesus is our entire list (and more) on any given day.

We cannot live the Word, apply the Word, pray the Word, know the Word, or even spread the Word if we don't first read the Word. And our capacity to apply the Word effectively will be equal to our willingness to wait long enough in the Word for the Holy Spirit to come and enlighten our minds in its promises.

Take God's Word today and make it a vital part of your praying. As you hold the pages open before you, you might wish to pray what John Calvin often prayed before embarking on his daily journey in God's Word:

O Lord, heavenly Father, in whom is the fullness of light and wisdom, enlighten my mind by Your Holy Spirit, and give me grace to receive Your Word with reverence and humility, without which no one can understand Your truth. For Christ's sake, Amen.[2]

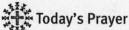

Today's Prayer

IT IS COMFORTING, FATHER, TO READ YOUR WORD, WHICH SAYS, "IF ANY OF YOU LACKS WISDOM, LET HIM ASK OF GOD . . . AND IT WILL BE GIVEN TO HIM" (JAMES 1:5, NIV). MORE THAN ANYTHING, OTHER THAN FORGIVENESS, WE NEED WISDOM. SOLOMON ASKED FOR WISDOM RATHER THAN RICHES. LORD, I'M NOT LIKE SOLOMON. I SEEK SHORTCUTS TO SOLUTIONS. I AM TOO QUICK TO SUPPOSE EASY ANSWERS ARE FORTHCOMING. BUT I'M HERE TO "ASK IN FAITH (FOR WISDOM), NOTHING DOUBTING." I BELIEVE YOU WILL GIVE ME WISDOM FOR TODAY, WISDOM FOR ITS DECISIONS, WISDOM FOR MY CONVERSATIONS, AND WISDOM FOR TOUCHING OTHERS WITH YOUR LOVE. I BELIEVE BECAUSE YOU HAVE MADE JESUS TO BECOME WISDOM FOR ME AND UNTO ME. AND IT IS IN HIS NAME I PRAY. AMEN.

MY PERSONAL MEDITATIONS

_____

_____

_____

_____

_____

_____

_____

_____

_____

MORE NAMES FOR JESUS

Check the index beginning on page 162 for these additional names for Jesus that suggest the Wisdom of God: Lawgiver; Wisdom; Wonderful Counselor.

The Bread of Life

Jesus replied, "I am the bread of life. Whoever comes to me will never be hungry again. Whoever believes in me will never be thirsty." John 6:35

The Japanese are known for the horticultural artistry of bonsai—the unique cultivation of dwarf trees. These exact duplicates of full grown trees possess all the features of their full-sized counterpart but in miniature.

As the seedlings grow, the Japanese gardener begins to stunt the tree's growth. They are transplanted to pots that do not contain enough soil to nourish their branches. Any buds are removed. Eventually the trees put forth no new buds, and remain dwarfs throughout life.

So it is with spiritual dwarfs, people in Christ's body who never mature in Jesus. E. Stanley Jones said, "I am better or worse as I pray more or less. It works for me with mathematical precision."

Christ said it this way, "People do not live by bread alone, but by every word that comes from the mouth of God" (Matthew 4:4). Loosely paraphrased, this might read—"No nourishment, no growth; no food, no fruit!"

Knowing His Name

John, who provides us with a variety of views regarding Christ's character through His names and titles, also introduces us to Jesus as the Bread of Life (John 6:35). It happens at the Passover meal that Jesus is sharing with His disciples. Jesus wanted to convey that He is the equivalent of the Passover lamb found in the Exodus account (Exodus 12). In that lifesaving circumstance, the blood of the Passover lamb protected God's people (Exodus 12:7, 13), and nourished them as well (Exodus 12:8). But Christ's disciples seem puzzled when Jesus says pointedly, "For my flesh is true food, and my blood is true drink" (John 6:55). Christ is saying that He has come to provide both deliverance and nourishment.

Living His Name

There are numerous mentions of bread in the Bible that give us insight into what it means to live daily in Jesus' name, the Bread of Life. In Genesis, the curse of sin from the Fall requires man to earn his bread or sustenance "by the sweat of [his] brow" (Genesis 3:19). But in Christ, who is our "living bread," salvation is freely given. We don't have to earn it; salvation is a gift (Ephesians 2:8). This suggests that living today in Jesus' name, the Bread of Life, is to live in the fullness of Christ as our Savior.

Later in Genesis we read of Joseph's management of the grain (bread) during Egypt's famine and loving care for his brothers as the famine reaches them (Genesis 41–45). Here again we see a picture of Jesus, this time as our Sustainer. As the Bread of Life, He is able to sustain us in times of deficiency.

In John 6:1-13, we find the account of Jesus feeding the multitude from what seems like a meager lunch. As the Bread of Life, Christ is never stopped by the limitations of a circumstance. No matter how insignificant a resource may seem, He is able to multiply it fully to meet our every need. He is our Supplier.

Scriptures that we read today in Jesus' name will come alive *with new freshness.*

Day 27 {NOURISHMENT}

Praying His Name

Christ refers to Himself as "bread" ten times in John's Gospel. On one of those occasions He specifically likens Himself to the manna Israel fed upon in the wilderness. (Compare John 6:32 and Exodus 16:4.) In God's gift of manna, we discover several unique insights that help us pray in Jesus' name, the Bread of Life.

First, *each day brought a fresh supply of nourishment* (Exodus 16:4). Nothing God has prepared for us is stale. Scriptures that we read today may have been written centuries ago, but in Jesus' name, they will come alive with new freshness. If we happen to be following a day-by-day Bible reading plan, we might even see how God has purposely ordered the readings so we would encounter certain verses on certain days!

Second, *that fresh supply of nourishment needed to be gathered every morning* (Exodus 16:4). A healthy habit of daily "feasting" in God's Word requires discipline. It doesn't happen by accident. To pray effectively in Jesus'

name we need to meet Him daily in His Word. Days spent without God's Word are weak indeed!

Finally, *each day required a new supply of divine nourishment* (Exodus 16:16-21). Israel quickly discovered God's principle of spiritual spoilage. Moses told them, "Do not keep any of it until morning" (Exodus 16:19). God is telling us that we can't live today on yesterday's nourishment. As the psalmist said, "Listen to my voice in the morning, LORD. Each morning I bring my requests to you and wait expectantly" (Psalm 5:3). David made prayer a daily experience. Little wonder God called him "a man after my own heart"! (Acts 13:22).

So tackle today in Jesus' name, the Bread of Life, knowing you've been nourished at His table. Prayerfully declare that He is your Savior, Sustainer, and Supplier in every area where you feel deficient. Above all, practice daily spiritual discipline to nourish yourself alone with Jesus, in His Word, before facing the demands of another new day.

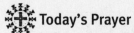

Today's Prayer

I AM LEARNING, FATHER, THAT THE BREAD OF LIFE ISN'T POSSIBLE "EXCEPT A
GRAIN OF WHEAT FALL INTO THE GROUND AND DIE." TODAY, AS I PRAY IN THE NAME
OF JESUS, YOUR GIFT OF THE BREAD OF LIFE, I AM REMINDED OF THE COST YOUR
SON PAID SO I MIGHT BE NOURISHED. I PRAISE HIM FOR HIS SAVING DEATH AND
REDEEMING LIFE, ASKING THAT THE SAME MIGHT BE MIRRORED IN ME AS I LEARN
TO LIVE AND PRAY IN HIS NAME. HELP ME. TEACH ME. SHOW ME HOW TO DIE TO
SELFISHNESS; THAT IN DYING I MIGHT BE MILLED IN THE PROCESSES OF YOUR WORK
IN ME AND LIVE TO BECOME A PERSON WHO NOURISHES OTHERS—THOSE PEOPLE MY
LORD JESUS WANTS ME TO TOUCH . . . IN HIS NAME. AMEN.

MY PERSONAL MEDITATIONS

_____

_____

_____

_____

_____

_____

_____

_____

_____

MORE NAMES FOR JESUS

*Check the index beginning on page 162 for these additional names for Jesus
that suggest the Bread of Life: Bread of God; Grain Offering; Living Bread;
True Bread from Heaven.*

28 {TOTALITY}

The First and the Last

When I saw him, I fell at his feet as if I were dead. But he laid his right hand on me and said, "Don't be afraid! I am the First and the Last."   **Revelation 1:17**

If you've ever taken any writing classes, you probably heard the instructor mention the importance of both the beginning of your story and its ending. A strong beginning draws the reader in; a strong ending pulls everything together and is gratifying.

That concept of a total picture is Christ Himself, the First and the Last—the Alpha and Omega. "All that exists," wrote François Fenelon in *Maximes des Saints,* "exists only by the communication of God's infinite being. All that has intelligence, has it only by derivation from His sovereign reason; and all that acts, acts only from the impulse from His supreme activity." The seventeenth-century mystic concludes, "It is He who does all in all; it is He who, at each instant of our life, is the beating of our heart, the movement of our limbs, the light of our eyes, the intelligence of our spirit, the soul of our soul."[1]

Christ is the totality of all we are and ever hope to be. He, alone, is the fullness of God's total revelation to man. And without this revelation mankind has no hope. As Søren Kierkegaard advised, "It is so impossible for the world to exist without God, that if God should forget it, it would immediately cease to be."[2]

Knowing His Name

Of all that Jesus is, He is as much "the Alpha and Omega—the beginning and the end" (Revelation 1:8)—as anything else. Christ has always been, and shall ever be, all in all.

This phrase, "the Alpha and Omega," is so often quoted that some of its significance tends to be lost. It occurs four times in John's Revelation and each time refers to Christ's totality as a direct revelation of God Himself. It is the one expression of Christ's nature that Christ Himself gave. He said, "I am the Alpha and the Omega, the beginning and the end" (Revelation 1:8).

The Book of Revelation begins with two references to this title (1:8, 17) and concludes with two of the same (21:6; 22:13). It is as if these declarations are placed by God as "bookends" at the opening and closing of John's Revelation of Christ and His ultimate triumph.

In Revelation 1:8 we note the emphasis is on Christ's eternity, that His essence embraces all of time: "I am . . . the beginning and the end."

In Revelation 1:17 the emphasis shifts to Christ's lordship: "I am . . . the First and the Last." Here Christ is declared to be the Head of the church, Who reigns among His people.

Finally, in Revelation 21:6-7 and 22:12-13, the emphasis is upon His reward. After all that can be removed is removed, Christ remains, wiping away tears, making all things new, giving from the fountain of the water of life to any who is thirsty (Revelation 21:4-6), and rewarding each person according to His word (Revelation 22:12-13).

Let's take a closer look at John's detailed description of Christ in Revelation 1:13-16. Christ wears a long robe (Revelation 1:13) which illustrates both His majesty and authority; He has white, snowy hair and fiery eyes (Revelation 1:14) depicting His wisdom and knowledge; His feet are of bronze and His voice thunders like the ocean (Revelation

Christ originates and creates all we need to start *our journey as well as finish it.*

1:15) illustrating His dominion and rule; He holds seven stars (Revelation 1:16, 20) as He stands in the midst of the seven candlesticks, picturing sustaining, controlling role in church leadership.

In short, Christ is the totality of power in our world, as carried out through His people. From start to finish, almightiness and all-loveliness are His. He rules and loves through His people—and He wants to unveil all of Himself to them.

The words *alpha* and *omega* are the first and last letters of the Greek alphabet and as such represent Christ as the beginning and the ending. But consider this quote from the Greek lexicon (Bauer, Arndt, Gingrich): "As a symbolic letter the Greek 'a' (alpha) signifies the beginning; the 'o' (omega) the end. The two came to designate the universe and every kind of divine and demonic power." In Jesus' name, our Alpha and Omega, exists all power in the universe. He existed before any other power (including demonic) and will continue after all such powers have been subdued.

Living His Name

Christ, the First and the Last (Alpha and Omega), is Lord over the very beginnings and endings of our lives. Today is His completely. Our concerns are in His control.

Christ likewise, the "author and perfecter of our faith" (Hebrews 12:2, NIV), is the initiator of life's every detail. He originates and creates all we need to start our journey as well as finish it. He not only authors, He perfects. Note how Scriptures frequently remind us of this reality:

And I am certain that God, who began [alpha] the good work within you, will continue his work until [omega] it is finally finished on the day when Christ Jesus returns.

Philippians 1:6 (brackets added)

I know the one in whom I trust [alpha], and I am sure that he is able to guard what I have entrusted to him [omega] until the day of his return.

2 Timothy 1:12 (brackets added)

Praying His Name

To pray in Jesus' name, the First and the Last, is to saturate our prayers knowing Christ alone is the totality of all we need. Getting answers to our prayers takes second place to meeting Jesus through prayer. He is the beginning and ending of all we could possibly desire. He is the ultimate answer to all our prayers.

Praying in Jesus' name, the First and the Last, means we infuse His fullness into every aspect of our days. We recognize that nothing escapes the sweep of His name. The "all and all" is with us. And because He controls all the power of eternity through His name, we need not fear any difficulty. Christ not only was with each of us in all our yester-days, He goes ahead of us into all our tomorrows.

Think of it! Tomorrow has yet to arrive, but Jesus is already there. He is our First and Last, and in Him we have the sum total of God's goodness. We can pray with Julian of Norwich:

God, of Your goodness give me Yourself; for You are sufficient for me. I cannot properly ask anything less, to be worthy of You. If I were to ask less, I should always be in want. In You alone do I have all.[3]

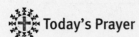 ## Today's Prayer

I COME TO YOU, LORD, CAUGHT WITHIN TIME. MY DAYS ARE TOO SHORT; MY TRIALS SEEM TOO LONG; SO MUCH OF LIFE SEEMS SCHEDULED BY A CLOCK I WANT TO CONTROL BUT CAN'T. I CONFESS MY SINS OF IMPATIENCE AND HASTE. I HAVE HURRIED INTO SITUATIONS AND CREATED WAVES OF CONFUSION INSTEAD OF BRINGING KINGDOM TRANQUILITY. I NEED YOU, LORD. YOU WHO TRANSCEND TIME— YOU WHO ARE BOTH THE ETERNAL BEFORE AND THE INFINITE AFTERWARD—COME FILL MY NOW. JESUS, ALPHA AND OMEGA, THE FIRST AND THE LAST, START WRITING WHAT SHOULD BE WRITTEN IN MY PRESENT CIRCUMSTANCES. HELP ME TO LIVE IN YOUR NAME—JESUS, THE FIRST AND THE LAST. YOU KNOW ALL THAT HAS PRECEDED THIS MOMENT AND WHAT SHOULD FLOW OUT OF IT, SO GUIDE MY PATH TODAY IN YOUR WISDOM AND FOR YOUR PURPOSES. THANK YOU, LORD, IN JESUS' NAME, AMEN.

Day **28** {TOTALITY}

MY PERSONAL MEDITATIONS

_____

_____

_____

_____

_____

_____

_____

_____

_____

_____

_____

_____

_____

_____

_____

_____

_____

_____

_____

_____

_____

_____

_____

_____

_____

_____

_____

_____

_____

MORE NAMES FOR JESUS

Check the index beginning on page 162 for these additional names for Jesus that suggest the First and the Last: All That Matters; Ancient One; Beginning; He Who Fills All Things; I Am; Lord of All.

The Cornerstone

The stone that the builders rejected has now become the cornerstone.

Psalm 118:22

In ancient times, the laying of the cornerstone was critical to the integrity of a structure. Once the cornerstone was in place, it became the unchanging standard from which all angles and measurements were made. Today, the cornerstone is more often a ceremonial stone, displaying the date the building was completed.

God has a plan of ultimate completion for His universe, and Christ clearly is the focus of that plan. Phillips Brooks, best known for his Christmas carol "O Little Town of Bethlehem," put this in perspective: "Slowly, through all the universe the temple of God is being built. And whenever, in any place, a soul by free-willed obedience, catches the fire of God's likeness, it is set into the growing walls, a living stone."[1]

Knowing His Name

That Christ is the centerpiece of God's eternal plan is emphasized by the psalmist's use of the phrase "the cornerstone" in reference to our Lord (Psalm 118:22). In the New King James Version, the phrase used is "the chief cornerstone"; in the New International Version it is referred to as "the capstone." In ancient Israel, this stone was placed at the very top of a building—a true headstone. Sometimes it even was made of a different material than the other stones to bring attention to its superiority.

It is because the material of the headstone might, on occasion, be slightly different that we understand the words: "The stone which the builders rejected has now become the chief cornerstone" (Psalm 118:22). Christ, the Stone, was rejected because He was different. He didn't fit their preconceptions or specifications.

The significance of this title of Christ, the Cornerstone, is twofold. First, it demonstrates that He completes God's working in our lives, and second, it signifies the way He surprises us with His methods. If it were left up to our human reasoning, we would preempt the possibilities God has in mind for us. Prayer in Jesus' name, the Cornerstone, cements in us this twofold reminder: We can be certain Christ will finish what He is doing in and for us, and we don't need to be able to figure out how He eventually will get the job done. He may even surprise us!

Other references to this aspect of Christ's person as the Cornerstone are found throughout the New Testament (Matthew 21:42; Mark 12:10; Luke 20:17). Peter and John referred to this title when they were forbidden by religious leaders to teach or speak in Jesus' name (see Acts 4:11). If anyone questioned whether they were referring to Christ, the question was answered in Peter's very next breath: "There is salvation in no one else! God has given no other name under heaven by which we must be saved" (Acts 4:12).

Christ will finish what He is doing in and for us.

Living His Name

Reminding believers that they were citizens of another land, Paul wrote: "So now you Gentiles are no longer strangers and foreigners. You are citizens along with all of God's holy people. You are members of God's family. Together, we are his house, built on the foundation of the apostles and the prophets. And the cornerstone is Christ Jesus himself" (Ephesians 2:19-20).

Here the apostle was picturing Christ as the central, focal, foundational point of reference in the building (and completion) of the church. And since we are a part of Christ's church, living today in Jesus' name, the Cornerstone, is to live in His power to complete all that He has begun within each of us.

Christ sacrificed His life to "complete" our salvation. His scars testify to our completion. Just as a message or date is often chiseled or engraved on a building's cornerstone, Christ's body also was "engraved" with scars showing His dedication to our complete forgiveness, redemption, healing, and salvation—today!

Sometimes cornerstones are used as time capsules. Memorabilia and messages are placed within a cornerstone in the hopes that future generations will discover them and remember the past. Similarly, all the fullness of God has been hidden in Christ, the Cornerstone, including God's infinite riches and immutable promises. As we live today in Jesus' name we rest in the fullness of His completion, for Paul said plainly, "You also are complete through your union with Christ" (Colossians 2:10). Whatever activity we are engaged in, we are complete in Christ.

Praying His Name

To pray in Jesus' name, the Cornerstone, is to think of areas that remain unfinished in our lives and call upon Christ's miracle capacity to "complete" them.

Do you have more intentions than completed projects? Do you have to work on a broken relationship? Today in Jesus' name, the Cornerstone, claim Christ's power to complete those neglected things in your life—especially the areas of total surrender and self-control.

Enabled by Christ, the Cornerstone, we can pray with Desiderius Erasmus, the fifteenth-century saint:

Sever me from myself that I may be grateful to You; May I perish to

myself that I may be safe in You;
May I die to myself that I may live
in You; May I wither to myself that
I may blossom in You; May I be

emptied of myself that I may abound
in You; May I be nothing to myself
that I may be all to You.[2]

Today's Prayer

HEAR MY PRAYER, DEAR FATHER, OFFERED IN THE NAME OF JESUS, THE
CORNERSTONE. I GIVE YOU ALL THE PLANS I HAVE FOR TODAY . . . AND FOR ALL
MY LIFE. LORD, PLEASE DEMOLISH ANYTHING IN MY LIFE THAT ISN'T TO YOUR
SPECIFICATIONS OR THAT DOESN'T MERIT YOUR SEAL OF APPROVAL. I WANT TO BUILD
UPON YOU, JESUS THE CORNERSTONE, KNOWING THAT YOUR SURPRISES ARE BETTER
THAN MY CAREFULLY LAID PLANS. HELP ME, O LORD GOD, TO NOT HAVE SAND UNDER
MY LIFE'S FOUNDATION. IN JESUS' NAME, AMEN.

MY PERSONAL MEDITATIONS

_____

_____

_____

_____

_____

_____

_____

_____

MORE NAMES FOR JESUS

*Check the index beginning on page 162 for these additional names for Jesus
that suggest the Cornerstone: Cornerstone; Living Cornerstone; Rock of
Israel; Stone.*

Day 30 {FINALITY}

The Amen

Write this letter to the angel of the church in Laodicea. This is the message from the one who is the Amen—the faithful and true witness, the beginning of God's new creation.   Revelation 3:14

Have you ever heard the "Amen" sung in a great cathedral? The resounding beauty and power of one word seems to soar to heaven itself. Even if you can't sing it, your "Amen" needs to be strong and purposeful as Martin Luther wisely observed. Commenting on his personal prayer, Martin Luther said, "Make your 'amen' strong, never doubting that God is surely listening to you. That is what 'amen' means. It means that I know with certainty that my prayer has been heard by God."[1]

Martin Luther was emphasizing that a bold "amen" was a statement of confirmation. It was an indication that the person praying truly believed his prayers would be answered. Because *amen* means "it is done," or "let it be so," to make this assertion boldly, according to Luther, was to declare with confidence that as far as the petition was concerned, the matter in question was settled by the petitioner's prayer.

"Amen" is another title ascribed to our Lord in Scripture (Revelation 3:14). Jesus Christ is our eternal "It Is Done!" His name speaks finality to every one of Satan's assaults. In one sense, Jesus' name is the very signature of God appearing on the bottom line of every claim we make. Make no mistake about it: God's signature over all creation is His Son, for it was by Christ that all things were created (Colossians 1:16, John 1:3). Christ, indeed, is God's divine "Let it be so!"

146

Knowing His Name

A description of our Lord, the Amen, is found in Revelation 3:14. We read: "This is the message from the one who is the Amen—the faithful and true witness, the beginning of God's new creation." This verse notes three distinct expressions of Christ's person: the Amen, the faithful and true witness, and the beginning of God's creation. Let's look at the first expression—Amen.

The word *amen* occurs seventy-eight times in the Bible: twenty-seven times in the Old Testament and fifty-one times in the New. Think about it. When we conclude a prayer with the expression "in Jesus' name, Amen," we are in fact declaring both Jesus' name (Jesus) and one of His titles (Amen). It is almost as if we were saying, "in Jesus' name, Jesus!"

Sadly, the word *amen* sometimes loses its intended meaning because of its common usage. But since saying "amen" can be the same as saying "Jesus," it should change our thinking.

Amen basically means "let it be so," or, "it is done." But this isn't wishful thinking, like "Oh, I hope what I have prayed really happens!" The actual force of the word *amen* is best seen in its translation in the Septuagint. When Jewish scholars translated the Old Testament Hebrew word for *amen* into what they conceived to be the Greek equivalent, they used the Greek word *genoito*. The literal translation of this is "Let this come into being; let it exist." In other words, when we prayerfully declare "amen," we invoke God's creative power.

Living His Name

To live today in Jesus' name, the Amen, is to declare, "God bring these things into being." As our Amen, Christ is the final authority on any situation or circumstance we may encounter. Christ alone establishes, secures, settles, and fixes the Father's will in each moment we live. It is His responsibility to put God's will in place, and He does so wherever people

As our Amen, Christ establishes, secures, settles, and fixes the Father's will in each moment we live.

pray, "Thy kingdom come, Thy will be done . . . in Jesus' name, Amen."

To live in the certainty of Christ, the Amen—Whom John calls "the Word" (John 1:1)—brings to mind Peter's statement in 2 Peter 1:19: "We have even greater confidence in the message proclaimed by the prophets." Peter is discussing the trustworthiness of God's Word given to us by His Holy Spirit. God's promises given in Christ are both assured to us as unshakably true and available to us ultimately, conclusively, and with final certainty. In Jesus' name, our Amen, our sure "Word" is firmly secured. Our "So Be It" says so!

Christ, the Amen, defines finality—in the end Christ's power will determine the outcome of every situation we face. We must live each moment in His "Amen power," literally His power to create. In His name there is an unlimited supply of this power; nothing in accordance with His will (1 John 5:14-15) can be stopped from being brought into reality.

This truth is further underscored by Paul's words in 2 Corinthians 1:20: "For all of God's promises have been fulfilled in Christ with a resounding 'Yes!'

And through Christ, our 'Amen' (which means 'Yes') ascends to God for his glory."

Praying His Name

How does this understanding of the Amen affect our personal prayer? *Every promise of God is imparted in the person of Christ Himself.* And because Jesus is the "Incarnate Word," when we pray in His name He becomes to us the "Confirming Word." Every promise we claim today in prayer is "amened" in Christ by God.

Think of it in these terms: As you claim a promise concerning a specific need and then declare that need in Jesus' name, it is as though the Father Himself says, "Amen . . . let the promise I have given now be fulfilled for the glory of My Son!"

Finally, when praying today in Jesus' name, the Amen, remember the context in which this title of Christ appears. It is found in Revelation 3:14, in a letter addressed to the church at Laodicea where people are being lulled by the idea that their own resources are sufficient for their needs. We hear them testifying " '[We are] rich. [We] have everything [we] want. [We] don't need a thing!' " (Revelation 3:17). The Lord, however, declares that the Laodicean church is impoverished, despite their appearance of wealth.

The message is clear: The final estimate of our worth is not what we have in our hands but what our Creator has to say. A person praying with the Amen on his lips is better off than a person with a large bank account. The latter's resource is temporal. The former, eternal. So, praying in Jesus' name, the Amen, is praying with the knowledge that Christ alone is the final authority in all those specific matters. As far as Christ is concerned, what we have claimed today in accordance with God's will is final. Christ's name assures it. God's sovereignty "amens" it. Therefore, it is done!

 ## Today's Prayer

AS YOU COME TO PRAYER TODAY, SELECT VARIOUS PROMISES FROM GOD'S WORD THAT APPLY TO SPECIFIC NEEDS YOU MIGHT HAVE. HERE ARE SOME EXAMPLES:

LORD, I COME WITH HIGH PRAISES TO YOU BECAUSE YOU HAVE GIVEN ME YOUR WORD, AND YOUR WORD IS TRUE. I COME TO STAND UPON YOUR WORD, AND TO LIVE WITHIN THE PERSON OF JESUS, THE AMEN. IN JESUS' NAME I SAY, "AMEN," TO YOUR PROMISES: "ALL THINGS WORK TOGETHER FOR GOOD . . ." "YOU WILL SUPPLY ALL MY NEEDS . . ." "YOU ARE THE LORD WHO HEALS . . ." "YOU DON'T WANT ANYONE TO DIE WITHOUT KNOWING YOU . . ." "YOU ARE ABLE TO SAVE ME FROM THE WICKED . . ." BECAUSE YOU HAVE SPOKEN YOUR WORD, BECAUSE YOU HAVE SETTLED IT IN HEAVEN, AND BECAUSE YOU HAVE GIVEN IT TO ME—I SAY, "AMEN!" AND IN SAYING "AMEN," I STEP WITHIN THE CIRCUMFERENCE OF MY LORD JESUS' CIRCLE OF POWER AND GRACE, KNOWING THAT HE IS YOUR WORD INCARNATE. ALL YOUR PROMISES ARE VERIFIED IN HIM, AND I AM LIVING TODAY IN HIM . . . AND IN THOSE PROMISES. THANK YOU, FATHER. IN JESUS' NAME, AMEN!

Day 30 {FINALITY}

MY PERSONAL MEDITATIONS

_____

_____

_____

_____

_____

_____

_____

_____

_____

_____

_____

_____

_____

_____

_____

_____

_____

_____

_____

_____

_____

_____

_____

_____

_____

_____

_____

MORE NAMES FOR JESUS

Check the index beginning on page 162 for these additional names for Jesus that suggest the Amen: Faithful and True; Faithful God; Lord Most High; Lord of All the Earth.

31 {MAJESTY}

The Glorious Lord

No, the wisdom we speak of is the mystery of God—his plan that was previously hidden, even though he made it for our ultimate glory before the world began. But the rulers of this world have not understood it; if they had, they would not have crucified our glorious Lord.   1 Corinthians 2:7-8

How many times have you been captivated by nature's beauty? Maybe it was a stunning sunset, a breathtaking view of a mountain or ocean, a garden or prairie bursting with colors. Did you catch yourself saying, "It's so glorious"?

Creation is a reflection of its Creator; all the beauty about us mirrors the majesty of God. Whether it's the tiniest snowflake or an immense galaxy, all of creation testifies to the splendor of Christ's "mantle of majesty." The psalmist writes, "The heavens proclaim the glory of God. The skies display his craftsmanship" (Psalm 19:1); and "The LORD is king! He is robed in majesty" (Psalm 93:1).

All creation is "window dressing" for Christ's excellence. It all points to Him. And just as a king's palace with all its royal furnishings reflects something of that king's personality, so creation reflects the magnificence of our Lord's nature and character.

More amazing is the fact that God, Who was clothed with majesty, chose to become the personification of majesty when He came to earth in the form of His Son, Jesus Christ. Paul wrote, "For God was in Christ, reconciling the world to himself" (2 Corinthians 5:19). Christ alone is the majesty of God wrapped up in a person.

Knowing His Name

Paul sums up this reality in referring to Christ as the Glorious Lord (1 Corinthians 2:7-8). The word *glory* denotes excellence. Jesus is not merely excellence, he's the Lord of Excellence. Clearly this is a reference to Christ's royalty as well as His splendor.

The Greek word *doxa* (from which we derive doxology) means brightness and radiance. We especially see this in 1 Corinthians 15:40 where *doxa* refers to the varied degrees of the magnitude and brightness (glory) of the stars and moon.

The sheer brilliance of Christ's majesty is really an outflow of the expression of Christ Himself as God. Scripture states, "God is light, and there is no darkness in him at all" (1 John 1:5), and Christ dwells in "light so brilliant that no human can approach him" (1 Timothy 6:16).

Yet the amazing thing about Christ is that He hid His glory. The powers of hell and of this world did not realize that this Man, Who appeared so weak because He humbled Himself on the cross, was in fact the Glorious Lord—the One "excelling" all! Christ was accomplishing an act that would be for our glory (1 Corinthians 2:7). Indeed, Christ hid His glory in order to make us recipients of His excellence.

Look at the tender and significant statement in Christ's prayer where He specifically asks, "Father, I want these whom you have given me to be with me where I am. Then they can see all the glory you gave me because you loved me even before the world began!" (John 17:24).

Jesus acknowledges two essential facts. First, *He longs for us to understand the splendor of His person,* and fully grasp the love that compelled Him to lay aside His heavenly glory to come to us. Second, *He wants us to share that glory with Him*, regardless of our position in society. Hebrews 2:10 emphasizes Christ's goal "to bring many children into glory." Here we see His love which causes us to be "raised from the dead along with Christ" where

Make a practice of declaring God's glory throughout the day.

we are "seated with him in the heavenly realms." This love is unending because "God can point to us in all future ages as examples of the incredible wealth of his grace and kindness toward us, as shown in all he has done for us who are united with Christ Jesus" (Ephesians 2:6-7).

The only other place in the New Testament where Christ is referred to as the Glorious Lord is in James 2:1: "My dear brothers and sisters, how can you claim to have faith in our *glorious Lord Jesus Christ* [literally "the Glorious One"], if you favor some people over others?" (italics added). What does this tell us? We need to be as indiscriminate as Christ when He sacrificed His life for the "everyones" of this world (John 3:16; Romans 10:13). He has invited us all to equally share in His glory. As a community of believers we are not to reject anyone because of social status or lack of special graces, gifts, or resources.

Chabod, the Old Testament Hebrew word for "glory," focuses more on the idea of weightiness than brightness. Something's worth or worthiness related to its weight on the scale rather than on how brightly the metal or gems shone. The Glori-

ous Lord, in this sense, is weighty in His worth, and by His very nature. He literally outweighs any value or force compared or opposed to Him.

What a wonderful message that is for us! Our burdens, transferred to Him, are as nothing to Him. All our sins are outweighed by His glorious majesty demonstrated in His death for us. Further, in any contest, the Lord "outweighs" every opponent. No enemy can withstand the force of Christ's person or the glory of His greatness as we take our stand in Him.

Living His Name

Jesus is not merely our glory (even our glory personified), He is the Lord of that glory. And because glory is excellence, this combination of terms suggests that Christ is the Lord of our Excellence.

What do we mean when we use the term *Lord* in reference to Christ? And how does an understanding of this expression help us live today in Jesus' name with greater authority?

For one thing, the word *Lord* (the Greek *kurios*) not only means "master" but "owner." The word *master* suggests "one to whom service is due on any ground" and *owner* includes "one who has the disposal or control of anything." Jesus is more than merely the Master of God's glory (excellence); He is the Owner of that excellence. Christ has at His disposal all that is excellent.

Thus, to live in Jesus' name, the Glorious Lord (Owner and Master), is to conduct all our business knowing that Christ is our excellence and majesty. All the glory of this day is His. If we receive any recognition today for any accomplishments, it really belongs to Him. Make a practice of declaring God's glory throughout the day. Since the majesty of our Lord is everywhere, our praises can be offered anywhere.

Praying His Name

To pray in Jesus' name, the Glorious Lord, is to saturate ourselves with His excellence and majesty in prayer. Paul told Roman believers: "Clothe yourself with the presence of the Lord Jesus Christ" (Romans 13:14). Never leave home in the morning before being "dressed up" in Jesus. Look at the list of some of the names of Jesus and prayerfully put them on! Tell the Lord you've chosen to wear His provision today, or His excellence, boldness, comfort, or confidence—or whatever else your day might require. As you say them, your trust increases. "Those who know your name trust in you" (Psalm 9:10).

Also take a moment to declare Christ your Owner and Master in all you do today. Identify a circumstance or situation and simply say, "Jesus, I declare You to be Owner of that circumstance," or, "Lord, I proclaim You are Master in this situation."

Finally, to pray in Jesus' name, the Glorious Lord, is to speak His majesty, His royalty, and His eternal excellence into the details, decisions, and desires of the day. It is to linger long enough with Jesus to catch some of the glow of His glory and then radiate His presence to others throughout the day. It is to be as Christ's disciples, who "saw his majestic splendor with our own eyes" (2 Peter 1:16).

Day 31 {MAJESTY}

Today's Prayer

DEAR FATHER, I COME WITH THANKSGIVING TODAY BECAUSE YOU SENT JESUS AS THE GLORIOUS LORD TO SHINE IN THE DARKNESS OF THIS WORLD. I PRAISE YOU FOR THE SHEER WEIGHT OF GLORY YOU POUR INTO MY SOUL AND EVERY SITUATION. TODAY I WANT TO LIVE IN HIS NAME—HE WHO IS THE GLORIOUS LORD. I WANT TO HAVE CHRIST'S RADIANCE SO I CAN BRING THE LIGHT OF JOY TO PEOPLE WHO ARE LIVING IN DIFFICULTY; MAY CHRIST'S LIGHT SPILL OVER THE BRIM OF MY LIFE IN SUCH A WAY THAT PEOPLE CAPTURE HIS WARMTH. IN HIS GLORIOUS NAME, AMEN.

MY PERSONAL MEDITATIONS

_____

_____

_____

_____

_____

_____

_____

_____

_____

_____

MORE NAMES FOR JESUS

Check the index beginning on page 162 for these additional names for Jesus that suggest the Glorious Lord: Blessed and Only Almighty God; Glorious Crown; Great King above All Gods; Jehovah-Elyon: The Lord Most High; King in All His Splendor; King of Glory; Our Glorious God; Our Mighty One; Ruler of All the Kings of the World.

Endnotes

Introduction

1. Andrew Murray, *With Christ in the School of Prayer*, rev. ed. (Springdale, PA: Whittaker House, 1987), 174.

Day 1: The Lord of Peace

1. David Manning White, *The Search for God* (New York: Macmillan, 1983), 309.
2. Veronica Zundel, *Eerdman's Book of Famous Prayers* (Grand Rapids: Eerdmans, 1983), 78.

Day 2: Wonderful Counselor

1. Zundel, *Famous Prayers*, 65.

Day 3: The Bright Morning Star

1. White, *The Search for God*, 228.
2. John Winnmill Brown, *Every Knee Shall Bow* (Old Tappan, NJ: Fleming H. Revell, 1984), 45.
3. White, *The Search for God*, 18.

Day 4: A Foundation Stone

1. Zundel, *Famous Prayers*, 33.
2. Ibid., 64.

Day 5: A Refiner and Purifier

1. White, *The Search for God*, 25.
2. Ibid., 305.
3. Zundel, *Famous Prayers*, 78.
4. Ibid., 18.

Day 6: The One Who Holds My Head High

1. White, *The Search for God*, 142.
2. Ibid., 228.

Day 7: The Radiance of God's Glory

1. White, *The Search for God*, 165.
2. Ibid., 54.

Day 8: The Hidden Manna

1. White, *The Search for God*, 195.
2. Zundel, *Famous Prayers*, 49.

Day 9: The Bridegroom

1. White, *The Search for God*, 43.
2. Ibid., 16.
3. Herbert Lockyer, *All the Divine Names and Titles in the Bible* (Grand Rapids: Zondervan Publishing House, 1975), 127.
4. Zundel, *Famous Prayers*, 41.

Day 10: The Rescuer

1. William A. Ogden, "He Is Able to Deliver Thee," *Great Hymns of the Faith* (Grand Rapids: Zondervan Publishing House, 1968), 201.

Day 11: The Sacrifice That Atones for Our Sins

1. White, *The Search for God*, 268.
2. Zundel, *Famous Prayers*, 62.

Day 12: A Wall of Fire

1. Zundel, *Famous Prayers*, 33.

Day 13: A Life-Giving Spirit

1. White, *The Search for God*, 11.
2. Ibid., 327.
3. Zundel, *Famous Prayers*, 81.

Day 14: The Lion of the Tribe of Judah

1. White, *The Search for God*, 139.

Day 16: The Power of God

1. Zundel, *Famous Prayers*, 22.
2. Ibid., 43.

Day 17: A Nail in the Wall

1. Zundel, *Famous Prayers*, 70.

Day 18: A Great Light

1. White, *The Search for God*, 133.
2. Ibid., 20.
3. Ibid., 135.
4. Zundel, *Famous Prayers*, 90.

Day 19: The Way, the Truth, and the Life

1. White, *The Search for God*, 41.
2. Ibid., 39.
3. Lockyer, *Divine Names and Titles*, 264.
4. White, *The Search for God*, 48–49.
5. Zundel, *Famous Prayers*, 113.
6. Ibid., 40.

Day 20: The Word of God

1. White, *The Search for God*, 10.
2. Zundel, *Famous Prayers*, 69.

Day 22: My Rock

1. White, *The Search for God*, 235.

Day 23: The Commander of the Lord's Army

1. White, *The Search for God*, 60.
2. Lockyer, *Divine Names and Titles*, 43.
3. Martin Luther, "A Mighty Fortress Is Our God," *Great Hymns of the Faith*, 36.
4. Zundel, *Famous Prayers*, 30.

Day 24: The Head of the Body

1. White, *The Search for God*, 46.

2. Ibid., 115.
3. Zundel, *Famous Prayers*, 51.
4. Ibid.

Day 25: The Expression of the Very Character of God

1. White, *The Search for God*, 264.

Day 26: The Wisdom of God

1. White, *The Search for God*, 288.
2. Zundel, *Famous Prayers*, 43.

Day 28: The First and the Last

1. White, *The Search for God*, 9.
2. Ibid., 47.
3. Zundel, *Famous Prayers*, 35.

Day 29: The Cornerstone

1. White, *The Search for God*, 27.
2. Zundel, *Famous Prayers*, 39.

Day 30: The Amen

1. Lecture notes from Change the World School of Prayer, Every Home for Christ, PO Box 64000, Colorado Springs, CO 80962.

Names of Jesus

All That Matters (Colossians 3:11)
Almighty One (Revelation 1:8)
Ancient One (Daniel 7:13-14)
Assurance of Glory (Colossians 1:27)
Author of Life (Acts 3:15)

Beginning (Colossians 1:18)
Blessed and Only Almighty God (1 Timothy 6:15)
Branch of the Lord (Isaiah 4:2)
Bread of God (John 6:33)
Bread of Life (John 6:35)
Bringer of Peace (Ephesians 2:14)

Champion Who Initiates and Perfects Our Faith (Hebrews 12:2)
Chosen One (Luke 23:35)
Christ Who Is Your Life (Colossians 3:4)
Coming One (Hebrews 10:37)
Cornerstone (1 Peter 2:6)
Creator of All the Earth (Isaiah 40:28)
Creator of Everything (Colossians 1:16)

Desirable in Every Way (Song of Songs 5:16)
Devouring Fire (Hebrews 12:29)

Eternal Life (1 John 5:20)
Exact Likeness of God (2 Corinthians 4:4)

Faithful and True (Revelation 19:11)
Faithful and True Witness (Revelation 3:14)
Faithful God (Deuteronomy 32:4; Psalm 31:5)

Flame (Isaiah 10:17)
Fortress (Psalm 18:2)
Fountain of Living Water (Jeremiah 17:13-14)

Gift God Has for You (John 4:10)
Giver of Victory (2 Samuel 22:51)
Glorious Crown (Isaiah 28:5)
Glory of Your People Israel (Luke 2:32)
God of Compassion and Mercy (Psalm 86:15)
God of All Comfort (2 Corinthians 1:3)
God of Love and Peace (2 Corinthians 13:11)
God Who Gives Me Life (Psalm 42:8)
God's Gracious Gift (Romans 5:15)
Good Teacher (Mark 10:17)
Grain Offering (Leviticus 2:1-10)
Great King above All Gods (Psalm 95:3)
Great Light (Isaiah 9:2)
Great Mystery of Our Faith (1 Timothy 3:16)
Great Shepherd of the Sheep (Hebrews 13:20)

He [Christ] Who Fills All Things (Ephesians 1:23)
Head of Every Man (1 Corinthians 11:3)
Head over All Things (Ephesians 1:22)
Holy (Isaiah 6:3)
Holy and Awe-Inspiring (Psalm 111:9)
Holy One (Isaiah 57:15)
Holy Sacrifice (John 17:19)
Hope of My Heart (Psalm 42:11)

I AM (John 8:58)
Immanuel: God Is with Us (Matthew 1:23)

Jehovah-Elohim: The Eternal Creator (Genesis 2:4-25)
Jehovah-Elyon: The Lord Most High (Psalm 7:17)
Jehovah-Hosenu: The Lord Our Maker (Psalm 95:6)
Jehovah-Jireh: The Lord Will Provide (Genesis 22:8-14)
Jehovah-Mekaddishkem: The Lord Who Makes You Holy (Leviticus 20:8)

Jehovah-Ropheka: The Lord Who Heals You (Exodus 15:26)
Jehovah-Sabaoth: The Lord of Heaven's Armies (1 Samuel 1:3)
Jehovah-Shalom: The Lord Is Peace (Judges 6:24)
Jehovah-Shammah: The Lord Is There (Ezekiel 48:35)
Jehovah-Tsidkenu: The Lord Is Our Righteousness (Jeremiah 23:6)

Kernel of Wheat (John 12:23-24)
King in All His Splendor (Isaiah 33:17)
King of All Kings (Revelation 17:14)
King of Glory (Psalm 24:10)
King of the Nations (Revelation 15:3)
King over All the Earth (Zechariah 14:9)

Lamb of God (John 1:29)
Lawgiver (Isaiah 33:22)
Leader among the Nations (Isaiah 55:4)
Light of Israel (Isaiah 10:17)
Light of the City (Revelation 21:23)
Light of the World (John 8:12)
Light to Everyone (John 1:4)
Light to Guide the Nations (Isaiah 42:6; Luke 2:32)
Living Bread (John 6:51)
Living Cornerstone (1 Peter 2:4)
Living One (Revelation 1:18)
Lord God the Almighty (Revelation 4:8)
Lord Invincible in Battle (Psalm 24:8)
Lord Most High (Psalm 47:2)
Lord of All (Acts 10:36)
Lord of All the Earth (Zechariah 6:5)
Lord Who Created the Heavens (Isaiah 45:18)
Love (1 John 4:8)

Master of the House (Luke 13:25)
Medicine in Gilead (Jeremiah 8:22)
Messenger of the Covenant (Malachi 3:1)
Messiah (John 4:25-26)

Mighty God (Isaiah 9:6)
Mighty One (Psalm 50:1)
Mighty Prophet (Luke 7:16)
Mighty Right Arm (Isaiah 51:9-10)
Mighty Warrior (Psalm 45:3)
Morning Light (Luke 1:78; 2 Samuel 23:4)
Morning Star (2 Peter 1:19)
My Beloved (Isaiah 5:1)
My Fortress (2 Samuel 22:2)
My Helper (Psalm 115:11; Hebrews 13:6)
My Lamp (2 Samuel 22:29)
My Lover (Song of Songs 2:16)
My Redeemer (Psalm 19:14)
My Rock (2 Samuel 22:2)
My Rock of Protection (Psalm 31:2)
My Servant (Isaiah 42:1)
My Strength and My Song (Isaiah 12:2)
My Support (Psalm 18:18)

One and Only Son (John 3:16)
One Who Guarantees (Hebrews 7:22)
One Who Rescues (Romans 11:26)
Our Glorious God (Acts 7:2)
Our Mighty One (Isaiah 33:21)
Our Passover Lamb (1 Corinthians 5:7)

Perfect Leader (Hebrews 2:10)
Personal Rescuer (Isaiah 63:9)
Prince of Peace (Isaiah 9:6)

Redeemer (Isaiah 59:20)
Refuge for His People (Joel 3:16)
Refuge to the Needy (Isaiah 25:4)
Renewer of My Strength (Psalm 23:3)
Resurrection and the Life (John 11:25)
Rich in Unfailing Love (Nehemiah 9:17)

Rock of Israel (Genesis 49:24; Isaiah 30:29)
Ruler (Micah 5:2)
Ruler of All the Kings of the World (Revelation 1:5)

Sacrifice for Sin (Romans 3:25)
Safe Refuge (Psalm 61:3)
Savior of the World (1 John 4:14)
Son of the Most High (Luke 1:32)
Source of Eternal Salvation (Hebrews 5:9)
Source of Hope (Romans 15:13)
Spiritual Rock (1 Corinthians 10:4)
Star Rising from Jacob (Numbers 24:17)
Stone (Matthew 21:42)
Strong Refuge (Nahum 1:7)
Sun and Shield (Psalm 84:11)

Teacher and Lord (John 13:13)
Tower of Refuge to the Needy (Isaiah 25:4)
Towering Rock of Safety (Psalm 61:2)
Triumphant Sword (Deuteronomy 33:29)
True Bread from Heaven (John 6:32)
True God (1 John 5:20)
True Light (John 1:9)
True Place of Rest (Jeremiah 50:7)
Truly Righteous (1 John 2:1)

Visible Image of the Invisible God (Colossians 1:15)

Warrior (Exodus 15:3)
Wisdom (Proverbs 8:12)
Wisdom of God (1 Corinthians 1:24)
Witness to the People (Isaiah 55:4)
Wonderful Counselor (Isaiah 9:6)
Word of Life (1 John 1:1)

Your Everlasting Light (Isaiah 60:20)